Letters to
a Young*
Playwright

Letters to a Young* Playwright

Practical and Impractical Advice on the Art of Playwriting

ADAM SZYMKOWICZ

APPLAUSE
THEATRE & CINEMA BOOKS

ESSEX, CONNECTICUT

APPLAUSE
THEATRE & CINEMA BOOKS

An imprint of Globe Pequot, the trade division of
The Rowman & Littlefield Publishing Group, Inc.
4501 Forbes Blvd., Ste. 200
Lanham, MD 20706
www.rowman.com

Distributed by NATIONAL BOOK NETWORK

Library of Congress Cataloging-in-Publication Data

Names: Szymkowicz, Adam, author.
Title: Letters to a young playwright : practical and impractical advice on
   the art of playwriting / Adam Szymkowicz.
Description: Essex, Connecticut : Applause, 2024.
Identifiers: LCCN 2024020483 (print) | LCCN 2024020484 (ebook) |
   ISBN 9781493088195 (paperback) | ISBN 9781493088201 (epub)
Subjects: LCSH: Playwriting. | Drama—Technique.
Classification: LCC PN1661 .S97 2024 (print) | LCC PN1661
   (ebook) | DDC 808.2—dc23/eng/20240513
LC record available at https://lccn.loc.gov/2024020483
LC ebook record available at https://lccn.loc.gov/2024020484

♾️™ The paper used in this publication meets the minimum
requirements of American National Standard for Information
Sciences—Permanence of Paper for Printed Library Materials, ANSI/
NISO Z39.48-1992

For Wallace

Contents

CONTENTS

CONTENTS

*A Caveat about the Title

I'm not ageist. This is a book for playwrights starting out or early in their careers. I'm using the title as a nod to the Rainer Maria Rilke book *Letters to a Young Poet*. In other words, I don't care how old you actually are. But, probably, if you're pretty far in your playwriting career you won't get much out of this book. David Mamet, put this book down. It's not for you.

Acknowledgments

I stand on the shoulders of the many teachers who taught me about writing and about a life in theater. I learned so much, too, from my playwriting peers, who are too numerous to list here. And from my students. Some of the teachers who changed my life and who taught me many of the things I'm going to say to you include:

Eduardo Machado
Kelly Stuart
Marsha Norman
The late Christopher Durang
Frank Pugliese
Leslie Ayvazian
Theresa Rebeck
Chuck Mee
Lee Breuer
Erik Ehn
Paula Vogel
Liz Bochain
The late Dr. Franklin S. Gross

ACKNOWLEDGMENTS

Tish Dace
The late Catherine Houser
David Lindsay-Abaire
Tanya Barfield
Jim Marlow

And many others. Whenever possible I credit folks within this book for ideas that are not my own, but sometimes I don't remember how I know something. Also, so much general knowledge is passed back and forth from playwright to playwright—who can say where it all came from? If I'm accidentally quoting you without attribution, I apologize.

If you are one of the teachers above, please know that I am grateful for all that you taught me. I can never properly thank you, but this is me trying.

Dear Playwright,

WHO AM I?

I'm assuming that if you bought this book you already know who I am, but maybe that's a dumb assumption. In any case, Hi. I'm Adam. Nice to talk to you.

I've been a playwright for more than twenty-five years with thirty published plays to my name. I have two graduate degrees in playwriting and have been part of many writing groups. I have a blog (aszym.blogspot.com) where I've interviewed over 1,100 playwrights. I've done a good amount of teaching in various places like Primary Stages, The Dramatists Guild, and NYU, and I have visited many, many classrooms. Additionally, I worked at Juilliard for eight years, supporting and sometimes mentoring the graduate-level playwrights there. I've also been married to another playwright for fifteen years. All of that is to say that I have spent many, many years thinking about and talking about playwriting at length. I have had thousands of conversations about writing and about building a career in the industry.

Over that time, I have picked up a lot of things I thought could be helpful to playwrights starting out. I often have coffee with newer playwrights and I find myself saying the same things over and over. So I thought I would try to get as much of it down as possible, here in this book. This is not a money-making scheme, this book. It's a gift. (Though unless you're getting it at a library or stealing it, you probably have to pay something for it.) But please know this is intended to be helpful. As such, please discard what isn't of use to you and take in what will serve you. We are all different.

Which also means everyone's path is different. I might hope for someone else's career, but I can't have it. In fact, there are no guarantees any of us will succeed. Careers rise and fall or never come into being. So many factors besides the effort you put in affect whether or not you can get a play up, or if anything more will come from a successful production once you do get it up. So much depends on timing, location, luck, and many other things.

Including privilege. I am straight and white and cis and male and fairly personable. I could wish to be taller or better-looking or wealthy, but I have a lot going for me. I worked very hard to overcome my social anxiety in order to meet a lot of people when I came to New York for grad school, because I knew no one at first. But I wasn't so introverted or paralyzed with anxiety that meeting lots of people was beyond me. I was lucky enough, too, to have great teachers—in the public schools I studied in as a kid, in the state school I went to for college, and in the fancier grad schools I was lucky enough to get into.

I think something else that helped me a lot was that when I was growing up, there were a lot of weirdos in my small town, and I think we were really given the leeway to be our weird selves. At least that was my experience. And my parents were both public school teachers so learning and reading were both valued at home. And I was in an enrichment program that started us on making and acting in plays at a very young age. I don't know if I would be a playwright if not for Ms. Bochain writing plays for us to be in and, later on in high school, the late Dr. Franklin S. Gross doing the same thing. I saw by their example that you could just sit down and write a play and then put it up. I still think about Doc

Gross at his electric typewriter, using whiteout to fix a typo or to delete a character when an actor had to drop out of the show.

So that's where I come from, but playwrights come from everywhere. Just look at the interviews on my blog to see the many different places people come from, and their many different approaches to writing. There are countless ways to do the thing we do. (There are probably over ten thousand playwrights at any given time attempting it.) You should do it your way. I'll tell you a little bit about my way and you can grab what you like—it's a buffet. There are a lot of things still I don't know, but here is a book full of things I do know and that I wish I knew when I was starting out. I hope you find it helpful. I wrote it for you.

WHY MAKE ART?

We make art because art feeds us. I think most people think the point of art is to share something with the world, to make people laugh or cry or think. To rewire someone's brain. That's valid. But I think that's actually the secondary effect of art. The main thing art does is for the *artist*—to make their life better. Everyone is different, but for me, my mental health is better on a day when I've written something. It helps my mood somehow, the act of expressing myself. And if I can get into a flow state where I'm writing but I'm no longer aware of time, that always centers and grounds me.

What I'm trying to say is that art-making, like exercise or yoga or getting a massage, is a form of self-care. If we have souls, making art nourishes our souls. And it's not really anything exclusive or magical. Anyone can benefit from making art, and you don't have to be any good at it in order for it to make your life better. Sometimes it's as simple as doodling on a page or writing an idea down in a notebook or whatever your version of this is: Strumming a guitar. Arranging rocks on a beach. Because also art is lots of different things.

Sometimes enriching your soul by making art is a slog. Sitting down to write is not always fun, but the more you do it, the easier it will become to slip into the flow state.

This is how I wrote about art-making in my play *A Thing of Beauty*:

AMY

We don't make art. Art makes itself through us. But we have to be
open to let the muse in. I mean the state of being where
it's not just us doing it. Time passes and you don't notice.
It's like you're in a trance. You come out and you feel like
you were led on by forces beyond you and just touched
God. It doesn't happen every time. For some people
almost never. But it's the reason to make something. It's
the dirty secret of why people are really artists. It's the
chance you get to commune. That high you get from creation when you're with the muse . . . Or with God or
whatever you want to call it. And you come out of it and
you're like how did I do that? It couldn't have been me. It
must have been someone else.

I think athletes know about it too. Scientists. Mathe-
maticians. They all know what it is to get in the zone. It's
just that for me, the way to that thing is through painting
. . . Or sculpting. But the muse won't come if you're thinking about your critics. It's why Fred doesn't read reviews.
It's why artists drink. That shuts up the critical voices for a
little while, at first, but it destroys you other ways I guess.
I don't know. I'm not an alcoholic. But I am addicted to
making art with my muse. If you could only access that
all the time—but you can't. Or at least I can't. But that's
the flaw of criticism.

You think the artist is creating something for you. But
she's not. She's feeding her addiction. The art is just the
byproduct of the process. The art is for the artist, not for
the people.

Some writers write to exorcise a demon inside themselves.
There is something dark and ugly and scary and by putting it on a

page they get it out of themselves, maybe get a little relief. While I write about things that scare me or make me angry, ridding myself of this internal darkness isn't the thing art usually does for me. But it might do that for you.

NOT MAGIC

But also, it's not magic. I think people who don't spend a lot of time making art think it's some kind of unfathomable mystery. There is the myth of the unknowable genius, and yes, maybe there are people who are very, very talented, but I think the concept of the genius doesn't take into account the work involved. There are no child prodigies of playwriting. Which is odd, actually, when you think about how much attention is given to young playwrights. But it takes a while to understand how to write a play. Sustained dramatic action is, I think, difficult to execute well in a full-length piece and it takes practice to understand how to do it well. It is very, very hard to write a good play.

But if you keep doing it, you can write a pretty good play and then a good play and maybe someday an excellent play. Some writers write their best work in their late twenties or thirties, others in their forties or fifties. Still others hit their stride later in life. Sometimes you don't know until much later what your best work is.

Playwrights are not magical beings. Art can be done well with time and practice. And talent is a factor, sure. But it's also just a lot of work. A lot of boring hours go into it. A lot of work unrelated to writing. A lot of prosaic fixes in rehearsals that have nothing to do with poetry. Which is to say: it is made up of a bunch of skills that can be learned.

WHY WRITE PLAYS?

I love plays. I think plays are important and playwrights are important. I think a theater piece can move you in a way that will stick with you your whole life. In fact, I'm really not even writing for the audience. I write for the actors, although I think people don't really know what I mean when I say that. The sensation of being in a play and saying those words over and over and feeling those emotions as an actor in front of people is really a different experience of the play than the audience has. Those words that you've memorized stay in you and become a part of you. If you're reading this, you were probably changed by a play you saw or were in. We know what theater can do.

A thing I like to do sometimes is ask a theatrical artist what their first theatrical experience was. For me I was in a play in first grade where Ms. Bochain had us create characters using alliteration: Woop lives in the water, eats wingnuts. And then she created a play for us to act out as these characters. It seemed like we were writing it together in class but really it was her creation. There were songs in it. Dances. It was a lot of fun even though it wasn't very long. I had a lot of theatrical experiences since then but that was my first.

YOU HAVE TO TRY STUFF

If you take nothing else from this book, please take this to heart. You have to try stuff. Life and art is all trial and error. We try stuff—new ways of writing, marketing our writing, meeting people, making a living. If you don't dare to try something new, you won't get anywhere new. You have to try stuff. Everyone has different external and internal forces that make doing some things hard. I don't pretend to know what your specific challenges are. Sometimes it's easy to take a blind leap and try something you haven't before and sometimes that's terrifying. You don't have to do everything this book suggests. But you need to try some things.

YOU CAN DO ANYTHING YOU WANT

In your writing, you can do whatever you want and no one can stop you. For example, this chapter is two sentences long.

ON DOGMA; OR, BE YOU; OR, SIGN THE PLAYS OR DON'T

I have a lot of published plays. One thing I like to do is go into the Drama Book Shop in New York and sign my plays. They put stickers on the covers that show that they are signed and then the books sell a little faster. If you're a customer in the bookstore and you're not sure if you want a play or not, the fact it's an autographed copy could be the tipping point for you deciding to get it. Or at least that's the thought.

When I tell other playwrights I do this, sometimes they say it never occurred to them it's something you could do. I get a good amount of logistical questions. *Do they know you're signing it?* Yes. *Do you just walk up to the counter with your books in hand?* Yes. And I always tell them the employees like it when you sign your books. And they do. The people in bookstores are nice. The Drama Book Shop loves playwrights. But other writers are maybe nervous to walk up with a stack of books and ask for a pen.

So I say to you, when you have a play published and in stock at the bookstore, sign the book or don't sign the book. It doesn't matter. Engage with your career on your own terms and at your own comfort level. Some people have email lists and some people don't. Some people do a lot of classroom visits and others don't. Find the things that you can do that help you and do those things. Very little makes or breaks your career. Don't be a jerk but otherwise, there is no play you have to write, nowhere you have to go. Showing up places helps a lot but also you don't always have to be everywhere. Do what is best for you and your art and your mental health.

Also, there is a lot of dogma around the right way to write a play. But I say to you, do what works for you and ignore the dogma. There are definitely things that work for most people and I'll tell you what works for me. What this book won't do is talk much about The Hero's Journey or the structure writers devise from it. There is already so much ink out there about that. It would be easy for you to find that online and in hundreds of books.

I will say that a lot of well-made plays are very good. Causation is helpful. This thing happening leading to this thing happening makes for exciting drama. Reversals are very helpful in drama— that is, "a change by which the action veers round to its opposite." (One of my teachers, Frank Pugliese pointed out that the play *Proof* has seven scenes and six reversals. It's a great play to study for structure.) A main character who wants something is very helpful. Conflict can be helpful. Plays without dramatic action are really boring—it should feel like something is happening on the stage. We want to be interested in what will happen next. We want to be interested in the characters and invested in what they are doing and what will happen to them.

All of that said, if we are engaged and enjoying ourselves, a play can be anything. If it works, it doesn't matter what rules you break. If it's not working, it's helpful to go back and look at the basics. Is there a main character who wants something and is prevented from getting it? Does this character change? Does the play you set up at the beginning get resolved in some successful way at the end?

But also write the play you want to write the way you want to write it. And if it's not working, try something else or write your next play. There isn't one single way to write a play and it's important to the theater to have lots of different kinds of plays.

BE YOU AGAIN;
OR, REALLY, BE YOU!

I think a valuable thing for an artist is figuring out how to be the most *you* that you can be. Early on, many of us imitate the art we are told is good or the art we love. But we must eventually find our own voice and that means accepting the specificity of our own lives and not seeing them as less than worthy. You must write about the world from your perspective. Where you are from is valuable. Your experiences are valuable. The way you see the world is valuable.

That doesn't mean, by the way, that because something is true in your life it is automatically dramatic or interesting. Reality has to be finessed to be good art. Some true things are not believable and some true things are just boring. But you need to write from your beliefs, your interests, what you know, what you care about, what you fear, what you imagine. Your dreams. What makes you angry? What excites you? That is what people really mean when they say "Write what you know." Find your wheelhouse. And as time goes on, figure out how to stretch your writing. Try new ways of writing you haven't before. Try things that might fail. But don't stop writing about what you care about.

It's sometimes hard to write about what is happening to you right now. It's hard to see what is important and unimportant while you're still in it. It's easier to write from the emotion of now but not necessarily about the specifics of now. A rule of thumb is that you may want to wait ten years to write about an event in your life. Also, some emotions that you carry around may have originated when you were a child or a teenager. That doesn't mean you have to write about that time in order to harness what it's like to feel alone or betrayed or in love or scared.

Marsha Norman likes to say, "Find your stuff." She tells students to find the thing you write "better than anyone" and write that. Many writers write a version of the same play over and over. Tennessee Williams is arguably someone who did that, very successfully. Not everyone does that. If you choose to keep writing about the same things, find another way to keep yourself and your audience interested. Write in new ways. Or write about new things in the same way. But definitely find things you really care about. If your heart's not in it, it will be very hard to keep writing and the final product will suffer. It's very hard to make good art if you don't care about it. Even when you're adapting someone else's work, you need to find your own way in. Or else it just won't come alive.

So write about the thing you most care about—what grips you like nothing else can. Write from your heart and your guts and let yourself bleed on the page. It's the way to make things that are alive.

ON ORIGINALITY

Many writers spend lots of time trying to come up with the idea no one has come up with before. I think that's almost impossible. There is no such thing as originality. Everything has already been thought of. But also, there is only one you, so everything that is wholly and completely you is original. So write from who you are right now and don't worry so much about coming up with a new take on something. Only you have lived in your body and grew up where you grew up. Your uniqueness is your starting point and what you care about and are interested in right now is the thing to write about. (This of course is not an original idea, either. My professor Eduardo Machado used to say a version of this and probably still does.)

The new idea is rarely really a new idea. On the other hand, finding a hook is helpful for marketing and for getting that first production. As far as I know, no one had ever before written a story in which "Robin Hood is and has always been Maid Marian in disguise" before my play *Marian, or The True Tale of Robin Hood*. But it's not a new idea. It's just a new take on an old idea: disguises are very common in Shakespeare plays and the other plays of that era. It hearkens back to that. And there were so, so many stories of Marian as a fighter and outlaw already. I just tweaked the idea and made a play about what I care about—love and being who you are and fighting for what you believe in. And it's one of my most produced plays, partially because Robin Hood is a known quantity that will get people to the theater and partially because it's about resistance in a way younger audiences can get behind. And it's fun and it's a good play, in my opinion.

You can do your version of that. But it has to start with you. I write a lot about women, I think, partially because I grew up with two sisters. I wrote about Robin Hood because I pretended to be Robin Hood a lot as a kid and watched lots of Robin Hood movies over and over. In Hollywood meetings they ask, "Why this story now?" and "Why are you the person to write this?" I hate both these questions, but I guess for my Robin Hood play I do have answers to both of those. I'm not sure they're good enough to satisfy producers. Maybe I wouldn't have been hired by Hollywood to have come up with a hypothetical version of Marian. But that's the other thing about writing a play. You don't need anyone's permission. You just do it.

STRETCH YOUR WRITING

I took a lot of writing classes at the Flea Theater in New York when I was a young playwright. A lot of experimental downtown playwrights were hanging around there learning and teaching. It was a great way to stretch my writing early on, in terms of both how I could do things in new ways and what else theater could be.

I don't take many classes nowadays, but I still try to think about ways in which I can write in ways I haven't before. I think this is helpful to all of us. What can you try that you haven't tried yet? My friend Sheila Callaghan used to read poems before writing as a way to open her mind and nourish herself and her work with a different kind of language.

Find what works for you. Is it meditation? Dancing? Do you write well with music on or with silence?

Paula Vogel has her students write impossible plays. What could you not possibly have onstage and how could you go about putting it onstage? Or: What in plays do you hate? How could you put the thing you hate in your play in a way that wouldn't make you hate it? (I feel like several teachers do a version of this task as an exercise.)

How can you collect things outside of yourself, finding language that is different from the language you typically use, and put them into your play? When I took a class with Chuck Mee, everyone in the class would bring in pages, and we were allowed to take things from those pages and put it in our own work. It didn't work well for me to take actual language from other people's plays, but I did take images and character traits and my play *Pretty Theft*, a play about stealing, came out of that class.

I'm not telling you to plagiarize. But use language you overhear. I think overheard conversations are fair game. Another thing I used to do is take some text I wrote and use Google Translate to translate into another language (I liked Korean) and then back again into English. Sometimes there were odd turns of phrase that I could adapt or change that were fun and would make my own words come alive in a new way.

Twice I have done silent retreats with Erik Ehn. He has us read poems, listen to music, and choreograph dances next to each other. We draw symbols. We make models and create rituals. None of these are things I normally do in my own writing practice and some of it works for me and some of it doesn't. It's out of my comfort zone. But I try. And I always write a whole lot in the silence.

Find your own things. Allow your writing to change and evolve as you change and evolve as a person. Be inspired by other works of art and find your own version.

LOOK FOR THE THEATRICAL

"Theatrical" can mean a lot of different things. There doesn't have to be a sword fight. (But can there be?) There don't have to be people parachuting on stage. The walls don't have to close in. Someone doesn't have to enter wearing a mask. Sometimes a thing is a play because the audience is inches from an engaging human relationship.

But what else can you do? My play *Hearts Like Fists* has a lot of stage combat, which can be super exciting. My play *Clown Bar* has gangster clowns shooting at each other. A lot of my plays have songs in them. A mirrored ball drops down in a prom flashback in my play *Kodachrome*. That play also has a photographer taking live photos that are projected on the back wall. Some of these can be done very effectively with almost no budget.

What do you like? I like it when it snows onstage. I like when things fall from the ceiling. I like transformations. Quick costume changes are fun. I like modern dance. I enjoy a night sky suddenly appearing. I like Christmas lights. I like shadow puppets.

Theater has a unique visual language. There are fun, non-literal things that can happen in theater that don't make sense in film. Find ways to activate your audience's imagination. When a play hints at something that isn't there, the experience of having to literally fill in the details can make it more exciting for the audience, in the same way that having to piece together unspoken subtext makes them more engaged.

ON MAGIC

I think beyond "the theatrical," we're all chasing that special moment when the lights and sound and costumes and set all come together, when the actor hits the exact right tone and the audience feels something intense in that moment, goosebumps or a shiver, a stifled sob—something that they will take home with them.

So much of this is luck. Having the right actor say the right words just right to make something special. And I hope at least once in your career you have a theatrical moment that feels like magic—where all the things come together and your work just soars.

I hope for that for you. Some people call it a religious experience. Maybe it is that. The whole goal is to help a group of people feel empathy, and we know from studies that people feeling empathy for a character increases the empathy they have for other people in their lives, and more empathy is really what the world needs.

So yes, your play can make the world a better place. Or if it's about gangster clowns, it can help people have a good time at least and give them some wacky photos to post on Instagram.

PLANNING YOUR PLAY

The first thing I do when I'm starting to write a play is answer Marsha Norman's five questions. They are:

1. This play is about _____.
2. It takes place _____.
3. The main character wants _____ but _____.
4. It starts when _____.
5. It ends when_____.

And then I use a simple structuring method that also comes from Marsha in which I try to come up with all of the scenes that a play like this might have and try to put them in order, finding cause and effect.

A simple outline is super-helpful before writing a play. This can change later on, but you have to try to answer the two most important questions: how does the play begin and how does it end? People will forgive things if you have a killer ending. Beyond that, what are the things that happen? What are scenes that will be in your play? Write them all down. Try to put them in order. If one thing causes another thing, great! That's the kind of thing your audience will expect from having watched a lot of TV and film. Speaking of which, why is this a play? Are there theatrical things that can happen that make sense in the world you are building? Visualize those. When and how can they happen?

This play is about _____.

What is this play about? What are you most excited about? There will be a time, maybe many times, when it will be hard to write. It's good to remember what excited you about the idea of the play in the first place. This doesn't mean it will always be as exciting as it is right this moment, but if you can grab even a spark of it, it may help you keep writing. This is also why you should write your first draft quickly. As time passes, priorities shift. We are interested in different things. We have different feelings. Write while the spark is fresh, preferably within a month or six weeks. Three weeks is better than six weeks.

Even if you don't immediately know what your play is "about," there needs to be that spark. Is it an image? A person? A place? What do you care most about? What lights up your imagination when you think about it? What do you feel in your bones? What is vibrating in you, eager to come out? What do you really care about right now? Or what are you terrified of? What makes you furious?

But also, eventually, you will try to get people to read this play, produce this play, come see this play when it's produced. What is it about this play that will excite other people and make them want to see it? It's okay if you don't know this before you start writing—that could even interfere with your process. But before you start the second draft, it is a helpful thing to think about. Can you put into one sentence what your play is about? What is the premise or the twist that makes us interested? Sometimes I hear what a play or film or book is about and I want to read it or see it just from that short description. In order for a theater to want to do a play, they need to know they can market it and get people to come. "Trust us, it's a good play" only goes so far.

Take a look at plays that are produced the most often. Theater Communications Group comes out with a list every year of the top ten most produced plays. A caveat: this list only covers TCG theaters, which are mostly but not exclusively the larger theaters in the United States. There are lots of other venues that are not TCG theaters. The Educational Theatre Association also compiles a list every year of most produced plays in US high schools.

For any frequently produced play, ask yourself: Is it being done a bunch because it won the Pulitzer last year, because it was an Off-Broadway hit and the *New York Times* told people it was a good play, or because it happened to be about something people cared about right now? Or does it have a really great premise? Does it touch on a recurring theme about humanity in a new—or seemingly new—way?

Study the synopses people write about these successful plays and try to write your own logline or short synopsis. What is the thing that hasn't been done yet, or what are you excited to explore? What is the best way to describe what you are making to get people excited about it?

But, also, if you don't think you can get people excited about it, is this something you want to spend months or years writing? You may still want to do it if you really care about it and you may find a way to get people excited about it even if you can't really describe it well. But know what uphill battle is ahead for hard-to-describe or hard-to-make-sound-exciting projects.

Sometimes an exciting premise will get a play done even if the play isn't great. Sometimes a theater wants a play about a certain subject and will do a good play about that topic instead of a great play about something else. So what your play is about is really important to its life.

But, also, what do you care about most? Love? Betrayal? Injustice? What are the stories about that you love most? Ideally, you want something personal to you that also touches on epic or universal topics. Everyone has felt guilty. We all have had our hearts broken. Most people can relate to stories about relationships between parents and kids. I write about grief and loss a lot and about love. Those are the things I care most about and what pull the strings inside me. What pulls the strings inside you?

It takes place _____.

Sometimes the setting is another character in the play. Sometimes it's incidental. This is a decision to make, where and when your play takes place. It helps you figure out the rules of the world of your play. If you are unclear about the world of the play, the audience will also probably be uneasy, wondering and thinking about things you don't want them to think about instead of continuing to be invested in the play. So the circumstances are really important to figure out. Some people like to draw a simple set and figure out where things are on the stage. Some people like to think of real places when writing and then make sure they can also be recreated on a stage after the fact. Do what works for you. Is this a play with a lot of settings minimally implied? Is it one place the whole time? Is there a theatrical set piece that's important to the play, like the truck in Nathan Alan Davis's *The Refuge Plays* or the angel in *Angels in America*? Is it *Our Town*'s bare stage? Or a Beckett wasteland? What does a lush version of your set look like, and if they have no money for a set, what would that look like?

What are the moments that the setting implies? What are the sounds that will come from the location? What kind of people inhabit this particular place?

The main character wants _____ but ____.

Look at your characters. Is there an "arc"? Do they start one place and get to another place? Are they changed? This doesn't have to happen, but this is one way to make a play that audiences find satisfying. Are your characters trying hard to get something? Finding out whether they get the thing they want and how that happens is usually why we're watching the play. We want to be entertained along the way, but the actual reason for us to engage is the situation and the objectives you set up with your specific world and characters. I want to know if and how they will get out of this mess. I want to know if they will find love. I want to know if they will get over loss. I want to know that tragedy is survivable. I want to know that people will continue. I want comfort. I want warnings of what not to do. I want my feelings affirmed. Or I want to learn new things. I want my world blown open. I want to be reminded what it is to be a person and I want to experience personhood through new people I've never met before. I want to laugh or cry. I want my emotions changed. I want to be a different person after the play.

Okay, all of that is a tall order. Not every play is going to be for every person. Some people want to laugh and go home. Others want to cry. Others want to be shocked. Some want to sing along. Your job is to make the kind of theater that you want to make right now. It could be sweet or violent or any number of things. Just be true to who you are right now and what you most want to make.

What does your character want? What is stopping them from getting it? How is that main conflict resolved at the end of the play? If it's a play that has multiple character arcs, fill out this question with all of them, even the small ones.

I bring up Marsha Norman a lot because she was my teacher for two years and then I worked for her for five more years at Juilliard. So I heard her speak a lot. She carries around a lot of wisdom. She believes that plays work best when there is one main character who has a strong want: the main character is the one with the most to lose. I write a lot of ensemble pieces but I have finally come around to her perspective. It always works best with one main character and one primary relationship. There can be secondary, tertiary, maybe even more ancillary plots and arcs and characters, but it's always best to have one main plot to anchor the play.

Likewise, Chris Durang saw how I filled my plays with wacky characters and shared a guideline that has stuck with me: There has to be a central person who is not wacky, who the audience identifies with. It's hard for the audience to find their way in if everyone's personality is oversized. It took me a while to embrace this idea, too.

It starts when _____. It ends when_____.

Think about the story you want to tell. What is its "container"? What is the moment you want to start on and what is the moment you want to end on in the timeline of these characters' lives? Sometimes the problem with your play is starting too early or too late. Sometimes you write multiple beginnings and you only need one.

Sometimes the play keeps going after the ending has come. The audience doesn't like that. Sometimes the audience is ready for the ending to come but there are a couple more scenes. Sometimes I have to cut those scenes out to get to the ending faster. Does the ending leave us satisfied? Has the goal you set up in the first five minutes been reached at the end? Are we in a different place than when we started the play? Have the characters changed?

Sometimes the problem of a play can be solved just by moving the beginning or the ending to a better place in the characters' timeline. I try to never start writing a play unless I know how it ends. Even if that changes later, it's helpful to have a good ending in mind to write toward. Maybe it's a stage image. Maybe it's very dramatic. The gun goes off. There's a devastating last line of dialogue. The metaphor you're building comes to its dramatic realization.

A good play with a great ending feels like a great play. A great play with an okay ending feels like an okay play. The right ending can make or break a play.

YOU DON'T HAVE TO KNOW EVERYTHING

Some playwrights think they have to know everything about the world of the play. Actors—especially inexperienced actors—sometimes ask a lot of questions about their characters that are unrelated to the play. That's great if they need to come up with facts and worldbuilding for their character, but you don't have to answer questions that aren't directly related to the scene. I tell them that's up to the actor.

In grad school, sometimes we would interview our characters to find out about them, writing a dialogue between the playwright and the character where we asked them questions. This was not helpful to me at all. I think it's helpful to think "What kind of person would do the thing this character is doing?" and then "Who do I know like this?" Make them similar to but also different in significant ways from people you know. I especially did this early on, modeling lots of characters on people I knew. I do this less now. Sometimes it's helpful to think of a specific actor when you write a part. I've done this a lot with stage actors I love. They never do it quite the way I imagined, but that doesn't matter.

You don't need to know your characters' star signs unless that's the way you categorize people. You don't have to know everything about them. You don't have to know what happens to these characters after your play ends. If people are wondering that, that's a great sign that you did your job of engaging the audience in the story. But you don't have to answer that question.

Almost everything I know about the world of the play and the characters is in the play. I don't write what happens after or before unless it affects what happens during the play.

Release yourself from the burden of knowing everything about your play. Yes, figure out enough so you can write it and understand it, but that's it. Life is too short to spend years coming up with backstory for a single play.

OUTLINING

You will save lots of time by outlining as much as you can before you start writing. Take notes on bits of dialogue, things you think will happen, or things you want to happen. It doesn't have to be detailed as long as you have a general idea of where things are going. Write down all the scenes you can and put them in the right order.

Not everyone outlines. Find your process and don't force yourself to outline if that's not organic for you. But know that if you don't outline, it's likely the writing process and rewriting process will take quite a bit longer than it otherwise would.

Whether or not you outline, though, when you write, be open to what the characters are doing that you didn't expect. Maybe you get to a moment you had planned out but it no longer feels like something they would really do, or they say or do something you hadn't planned and the play heads in a different direction. Or there's a scene that is missing that you now have to write, or a scene you no longer need. Maybe a new character appears. Maybe it turns out the play is about something different than what you thought it was about.

GIVE YOUR CHARACTERS NAMES AND GIVE YOUR PLAY A TITLE

Make up names for your characters. You can find baby names online and in books. Sometimes I use the same names over and over. Sometimes I like to use names I've never heard before. I like names that are shared by a lot of people I know, and I like names that belong to no one I know. I use the names Mark and Susan a lot for some reason.

It's important to give your characters names so you can start figuring out who they are. I think the earlier you give them names, the better. For me, it's hard to change their names later, but I have done it, including times when I gave someone the name of a real person they were based on and then changed it before the play went up.

I think choosing names, like choosing a title, is instinctual. Your idea of who Phoebe is will be different than mine. Choose a name that best expresses the character you're trying to create.

I have some plays where I knew the title right away and other plays where I tried a bunch of titles. There are literal titles like *Clown Bar* and there are metaphorical titles like *Cat on A Hot Tin Roof*. The title of *Proof* has multiple meanings. It's helpful if your play's title is evocative of the kind of play it is. The less we can glean from the title, the more lifting you will have to do in the description. But there are great plays with terrible titles. Don't worry if you can't find the right one right away.

Titles and character names are personal and shouldn't be decided by anyone other than you. When you find the right names, you'll feel it. But don't get stuck finding the perfect name or perfect title, or in doing lots of research. It's easy to procrastinate when writing the play by doing other stuff and then time passes and you still haven't written a play. Know their names. Know the answers to the five questions. Follow your feelings and WRITE THE THING.

SIT DOWN TO WRITE

Give yourself a goal for every day that you're writing. It should be achievable. When I was starting out, I was trying to write three play pages a day. There are days now where I write one really good half of a page and feel good about it. Other days I've written half a play in a day. If you write one page a day, it'll take you three months of working every day to write a ninety-minute play. If you can do two pages, you'll halve that time. Three pages, and it's done in a month. Maybe you write faster or slower than that. Maybe you only write one day a week or you write for hours on the weekends. Just find your time and put it aside and then after you're done, reward yourself for your work that day. Watch that show you've been saving or eat that chocolate. Celebrate the time you put in.

Maybe sitting for an hour is the way you measure your progress. Shut off your Wi-Fi or go off with your notebook and write for a certain amount of time. Thirty minutes can be plenty if you're actually writing during that time.

Some days you'll feel bad about how writing went. Other days you'll feel good about it. Either way, congratulate yourself on every day you get some creative work done. Outlining counts. Making notes on your play counts. Even research counts, but some people do too much research to put off writing the play.

THE WALL

About ⅔ to ¾ into writing your play, you may hit a wall. You'll have to push through and finish the play. It's okay if you write it badly. Sometimes your subconscious will tell you to stop writing the play you're writing and write this new thing it's really excited about. Take notes on the new thing. Write down everything you can about the idea, but then write the play you're writing. Keep writing through to the end. The alternative is that you won't have a finished play. It's easy to never finish anything. But you need to finish things so you have things to revise, to put up, to work with and work on. Keep writing to the end.

Some people can write multiple plays at a time, toggling back and forth between different projects. I've only done that a few times. It doesn't work well for me. If that's what works for you and you can finish plays while doing that, great! Ignore my advice and do it your way.

PERSISTENCE

One of my mentors, Tish Dace, stressed the importance of persistence for artists and writers, and it has been one of the most helpful guideposts for my career. Like in a play where your main character has obstacles preventing them from getting what they want, a playwriting career is rife with rejection and failure. The answer? Keep going. Keep writing. Keep sending your work out there. Create writing groups. Show up to your writing group with your ten new pages. Feed your friends and ask them to read your new play out loud in your living room. Write. Submit. Write some more. Self-produce if you can. See plays. Read plays. Whatever you do to feed your artistic life, keep doing it.

Really. So much can come by steadily doing something day after day. Which is not to say you have to write every day. You don't. Just keep at it. On your own schedule. Which brings me to consistency.

CONSISTENCY

Sometimes you may not feel like writing. And look, you never have to write, but I think sometimes it's helpful to sit down and write even when, or especially when, you don't feel like it. Get a few words down. Maybe a few more. Maybe you'll think of something you haven't thought of before. And then if it's not working, get up and take a walk. Forget about it. Do something else, but come back to it in an hour or a day or a week.

The only way to have a career is by writing things. And the only way to write things is to sit down and write things. I don't write every day. Most weekends I don't have time and life gets in the way. I'm not saying I write every day or even most days. I would say I write a little bit half of the time. And that little bit turns into a lot of plays every year. Or else I go off on a writing retreat for a few days or a week and I write a whole lot in a short period of time. Or I do a big revision. Everyone is different. Figure out what works for you. And then do it.

Maybe you write best at night, or in the morning. Maybe you can write on your lunch break or on the train to work. Find your thirty minutes or hour and try to figure out the next part of what you're working on.

A little bit consistently adds up to a whole lot.

And you don't have to always be writing. Sometimes I want to do research or want to plan what I'm writing. And that's part of writing too—just a different part. But eventually that has to end and you have to sit down and write. Or stand. Maybe I should get a standing desk.

Paula Vogel and Marsha Norman have both talked about how a first draft should come out quickly. Write it, if you can, before too much time passes and your priorities or interests shift. Finish it before your internal critic tells you to work on something else. Or ignore them long enough so you can finish. Get to the end. And then figure out what you have. Hear it out loud. Revise it. Hear it in front of people. Revise it. Maybe hear it in front of people again. Revise it. Try to get it produced. And while you're doing that, write a new thing.

WHAT IS GOOD?

We can't all agree on what is great or even good. The work of art you adore has scores of people who hate it. Name any play you think is a perfect play and I can find someone who can tell you lots of things wrong with it. This is okay. First of all, we all don't need to like the same things. People should be different. We have different lives, different experiences. But more importantly, a perfect work of art doesn't exist. Some writers will revise and revise and revise to try to achieve perfection. And you definitely should try to make your thing as good as you can, but perfection doesn't exist and good or good enough is all we can hope for most of the time. Put it out in the world and have it be good. Don't let everything sit on your shelf. You never learn anything that way and you and your work won't become better.

Now you also might not think your thing is good. Or some days you may hate it and other days love it. You may see only the flaws, or what you perceive as flaws. This is all normal. Unfortunately it comes down to you to get your thing out into the world. No one will do it for you. So make it as good as you can and then advocate for it like you don't know its flaws. Good writers always see how their thing could be better. Bad writers think their thing is perfect. Our goal is to improve and sometimes that means rewriting and sometimes that means putting it down and writing the next thing.

Also, don't get stuck on being a good writer or bad writer. Just try to be a better writer. And know that sometimes your best play might be something you wrote five years ago but you still need to keep writing because your next thing might be your new best work. It has happened to me many times in my career. And also, of course, it's completely subjective and the more you get stuff out in the world the more you will have people who prefer one play over another, who really respond to one particular work. What you decide is your best work can be your best work today, but tomorrow it can change.

No matter what, I promise you the play you are most proud of writing will get rejected, probably over and over and after it goes up will get at least one bad review and most likely more than that. Rejection happens at all levels. The most phenomenal plays get terrible reviews. So find a way to not rely on external validation. It feels wonderful when someone tells you how much your play means to them. It feels ten times worse when someone posts online how much they hate your play. Your value as a person can't be dependent on either of these people. You will go mad.

That doesn't mean these things won't affect you. But figuring out how to not derail your day or your week or your art is the most important thing. I'm not sure what methods will work best for you. Maybe ask your therapist for tips. But I think it's helpful to realize all of us who make art have to deal with rejection over and over. You are not alone. And even when you someday hopefully create a masterpiece, it will not be immune to derision. In fact, it's likely you'll get more pushback, as people feel like they have to overcompensate for other people's praise.

THINGS HELPFUL
TO KNOW ABOUT
BESIDES PLAYWRITING

I started out as an actor in school plays and I was in a lot of them, all through college, before I stopped doing that. Actors make good playwrights because you already know what works onstage. You've played actions. You understand what is theatrical. You've already felt the energy from an audience when something is working and when it's not. I often try to write parts in plays I think would be fun for actors to do. I recommend all playwrights take an acting class at some point or be in a play, even in a small part. You'll realize how hard acting is.

And if you can, do other things backstage too so you understand the amount of work and expertise that goes into a production. Lights, sound, costuming, set design, building. Stage management. These are all things people dedicate their lives to doing well. Talented designers and builders will make your show come to life. And your production stage manager makes the show run.

A basic understanding of what all these folks do will help you know what can and can't happen onstage.

PEOPLE DROP OUT

Keep at it. Lots of people stop writing plays. People leave theater all the time. So many people who went to grad school with me for playwriting don't write plays anymore. And if they found a fulfilling life doing something else, we should be happy for them. Like I said: it's hard. But if you keep writing and submitting year after year there is usually an effect. Most of us don't have the career we want, but lots of us have careers. (Which is not to say a living, necessarily.)

But also, if you don't want to be a playwright, don't be a playwright.

It is sometimes hard to work up the momentum to do another round of submissions or to start writing for the day. But doing this thing is about continuing to do this thing, so figuring out how to get your own ball rolling is important.

The world is not going to tell you they want a new play from you even if that's what the world needs. Some of the most celebrated plays were rejected over and over before finally being produced. Pulitzer Prize winner *Wit* is a famous example of this. Even the most successful plays sometimes have a long, hard road, which means the playwright has a lot of tough times, too. And there's so much silence, no matter how many submission you put out into the world. As Tom Petty said, "The waiting is the hardest part."

READ PLAYS

You need to see and read a lot of plays to understand what a play is and a play isn't. I think the biggest shortfall I see in young writers is that they don't know a lot of plays. Seeing plays can be expensive. Buying lots of plays can be expensive. And libraries that aren't in cities or well-resourced colleges don't have a lot of plays. So I sympathize and understand, but it's also really helpful to read good plays if you want to write a good play.

Get on the email lists of the major play publishers so you see what new plays are coming out. If you don't live in New York, take a trip there and see some plays Off-Broadway. Go into the Drama Book Shop and ask for advice on plays about a certain topic or style. Say, "I really love this play. What other plays are like that?" Read all the plays by a writer you like. Read the classics. Read the newest plays. And study them. Go to the New York Public Library for the Performing Arts at Lincoln Center and watch films of plays; they have almost everything. Join TDF or whatever they have in your area to get play tickets for cheap. Offer to usher to see plays for free at your local theater. Use student discounts or senior discounts. Ask what discounts they have. If you buy day-of, is it cheaper?

It's a major problem that many theatermakers can't afford to see theater as much as they'd like. I have no solutions to how much real estate costs and how much that drives up ticket prices. Just know that reading and seeing plays is really important if you want to write plays.

Also, if you possibly can, spend time working in the literary office of a theater. When I was in grad school, I interned for an agent, a producer, and a theater. In each role, for which I was paid very little, I read lots of new plays. I also had the chance to see how theaters chose seasons, went to lots of readings, and talked about plays with people whose job it was to read plays and go to readings. There is so much good work out there and so much more bad work. The more that you can experience, the better frame of reference you'll have for your own work. And you can better understand what you can and can't do on a stage, which is important in order to make new and interesting things.

Get *American Theatre* magazine from the library and you can read all the plays they publish. There's an index on their website of which plays are in what issue—though only some issues have plays in them. If you do nothing else, read those plays.

ALSO, READ OTHER THINGS AND LIVE LIFE

Knowing plays is helpful and important, but you should also read what you're interested in. You need to have things to write about and that means living a life and following your interests. You can never know what your next play will be. It could be from an article you read or something you see on the street at 3 AM. It could be from a bad breakup or from your day job that you hate. Read books about things you're interested in. Take trips. Experience things. Take yourself on artist dates to a museum or concert or to the ballet. Live. And continue to be a student. Stay curious—it will enrich your life and give you ideas.

NOTEBOOKS

Carry a notebook with you. Write down ideas you have, or overheard conversations. Maybe do "morning pages"—stream-of-consciousness writing done when you first wake up. Have paper next to your bed so you don't have to get up to write down ideas that keep you awake or that you have in the middle of the night. Keep a journal or diary. During the pandemic I started writing down the things that were happening in my life and in the news, partially to remember and partially for the release of writing things down.

I would not recommend buying the number of notebooks I buy. I will never fill all the notebooks I have bought for the purpose of writing in. It's aspirational notebook purchasing. For years I wrote in composition books that I covered with homemade collages. I found giant hardcover art books that I used to make big outlines for plays and screenplays. I started doodling a lot ten years ago, so now that's part of my process too. I use Post-Its. I use whiteboards and blackboards. I use typewriters. I have pen preferences. Sometimes the specifics of being a writer are ridiculous. Every writer I talk to has their notebook preference. Find yours. Is it a Bic pen and a yellow legal pad? Is it Leuchtturm and a felt-tip pen? Midori? Muji? What size do you like? Do you use gel pens? I have spent way too much time looking up notebooks online. But I also use a lot of notebooks.

NOTEBOOKS

I have boxes full of notebooks I wrote in, going back to when I was twenty or so. They are all full of notes on writing, ideas, thoughts, bad poetry. They were the soil that the plays I wrote grew out of. I have a fantasy that some library will want to acquire them someday for their collection, along with old revisions of scripts that I have scribbled on and held onto. But probably, when I die, my son will just throw it all away.

WRITING BY HAND

There is a reason I bring up notebooks. Yes, you can totally leave yourself voice memos instead or fill up your notetaking app with ideas. I often email myself ideas when I'm out and about. However, I would advise using a notebook, too, whenever possible.

There have been studies that have found writing by hand on paper lights up more of your brain. It may actually help you think better to write in a notebook. It may help you remember better. It may help you be more creative, come up with more ideas, make connections.

So write, draw, doodle, fill up notebooks with bits of ideas, things people say, images that come to you, fears. Collect these things. Try the exercise where you don't stop writing. Just start and don't stop for five or ten minutes or an hour. At the beginning, you may just write "I don't know what to write" over and over, but keep going and it may help you get to something you want to work on. I sometimes would write gibberish poetry until something clicked and I would find the thing I was trying to say or a solution to a moment I was stuck on in my play.

If you write scenes down on paper first, when you type it up you can make small revisions as you go and your first draft will technically be more like a second draft. Bring ten pages to a writing group and revise from what you hear there and then keep writing. This way, your first draft can sort of be at the level of a third draft—if not at the large-scale structural level, then at least within the scenes.

Sometimes, during the planning stages, I will sit down and try to figure out what my play is on paper and bits of scenes will pop into my head, locations or images. And when I've collected enough of them, I will have a better idea of what the play wants to be and will be able to start to write.

GENERATING IDEAS

The question I am asked the most when I visit a classroom is "Where do you get ideas from?" Or, "What was the inspiration for this play?" And that's tricky because ideas come from all over and maybe the play was something that came out of nowhere or something I'd been thinking about for twenty years. What they really want to know is, "How do I get good ideas?"

And you should figure this out on your own. Do you get ideas from sitting in a cafe surreptitiously watching people? Do you get them from reading articles and books? Are you inspired by dance or visual art? What inspires us is deeply personal but it's worth chasing and finding what excites you.

For years I would paint one thumbnail with nail polish. I don't know why I did this. For some reason it inspired me and made me feel like myself. I didn't like painting a whole hand. Just one thumb, usually black or blue or green. Nowadays it's a lot more common for men to wear nail polish but when I started doing it, it wasn't. I tell you this only because I think it was part of my artistic process at that time. I don't know why. Things are mysterious. Find your own mysterious things. Does it help you to write if you put on a costume? I wore a clown nose when I was starting to write *Clown Bar*.

Tactile sensations like taking showers or sitting in front of fans can be helpful for generating ideas. Getting up and taking a walk will sometimes break something open for you. In fact, all kinds of exercise can work. Running, swimming, whatever you like to do.

Meditation works really well for some people. For me, running sometimes serves the same function of emptying out my head for a bit. Sometimes, when you empty it out, new thoughts show up that are helpful. Do you write down your dreams? Sometimes your subconscious has useful things to tell you. I want you to enjoy the mystery that is you. Even if you think you know yourself pretty well, I bet there are things about yourself you don't understand. Actively seek those things out. Find ways your mind works and work with it, not against it.

Are you someone who needs a deadline? Set up a reading of your work in progress. Maybe the pressure of having people show up to read something helps you finish writing it the night before.

Have you tried writing first thing in the morning? I mean before you do anything: just open the computer or pick up the notebook and start writing. I don't remember who told me this, but for many of us, the internal critic just isn't awake yet and you can get a good amount of writing done before they wake up.

Do you write best at night or in the morning or the afternoon? Do you work best if you wake up in the middle of the night? Do you need a window to look out of? Do you work best standing up? Do you need no distractions or lots of distractions? Do you need a rotting apple core in your desk drawer, like the poet Friedrich Schiller? Ibsen famously put up a photo of Strindberg over his desk and claimed he couldn't write a word without "that madman staring" down at him. Do you need coffee to get your words going? Does it help to listen to music or is silence better? I found something called "Deep Focus Music" on YouTube that I would play when I was writing a novel—something much more difficult for me than writing plays. I think it helped. What helps you? Do you need a chocolate sitting on your desk that you get to eat when you've written your daily goal?

It's okay to do something weird to get the ideas flowing. Or maybe just take a walk.

TEN-MINUTE PLAYS

It's really hard to write a really good ten-minute play. But it's easier for a lot of us than writing a good full-length play. Early on, a lot of young playwrights write a lot of short plays. Some writers are really good at the short form. Don't worry if you're not good at short plays. It won't hurt your career.

It is usually easier to get a short play up somewhere than to get a full-length play up. Sometimes a theater will ask you to write a ten-minute play for them. A theater recently asked me for one about baseball. I literally have nothing to say about baseball and I had to tell them that. Now they're producing a full-length play of mine so I guess it didn't hurt me much to tell them no.

If you want to write a lot of short plays and send them out and try to get them up, that's great. There is a limit to how much a short play can do for you. But it can be a calling card at a theater, something to introduce you to some theater people. If you contribute to a night of short plays, you can be part of a community.

It's very hard to make a career from short plays. David Ives was maybe the last person to do that. Rich Orloff also excelled in that arena. I do have nights of short plays that get done in community theaters and schools. I'm not saying they're worthless. But they aren't done as much as they used to be and the publishers, in my experience, are less interested in them than they used to be too. Sketch comedy is still going strong and I know there are still some very successful musicals and plays that are a series of short plays or sketches.

A while back I decided to stop writing and sending out ten-minute plays and concentrate on full-lengths. It's a lot harder to get full-lengths up, but I think that decision was a good one and led to more productions of my longer work. I still write short plays sometimes, or short films if I'm asked to, but they're one-offs. For me, the rewards weren't worth the effort. But I think early on it's really a great way to see your stuff on its feet more often and that's the goal in order to become a better writer.

I have also sometimes written short plays that grew into a full-length: I tried something out that I discovered I wanted to work on for a longer period of time. Monologues can also serve that function.

BEING IN REHEARSAL

Playwrights are unique in that there's never more than one of us in the rehearsal room. Directors sometimes have assistant directors who are themselves usually directors in training. This is less common for playwrights. So, often, a new playwright may have never seen how another playwright acts in a rehearsal room. I also have not been in a lot of other people's rehearsal rooms, but I think I do well most of the time in my own rooms so I will tell you what I do and maybe it will help.

I talk very little during rehearsals. It's in my nature not to talk a lot but that's especially true for me when in rehearsal. This, I think, is helpful. Don't give notes to actors except through the director. Ideally, give these to the director when actors are not in the room and cannot hear you so they won't know which notes come from you. This is not always possible but try very hard not to give any note directly to an actor. The primary reason for this is that things you say about the play carry a lot of weight, and in first rehearsals everyone may be still learning what works and doesn't work. It's easy to lead them down a wrong path by saying the wrong thing or saying something the wrong way. Going down the wrong path is sometimes part of the process, but when a playwright leads them there it can take longer to get them back on the right path because of the weight that your words about the play carry. Which means when they ask questions about the play, be very careful what you say. It's also okay not to answer some questions or to tell them that's an actor choice.

You also don't want to undercut the director, which is another important reason not to give notes directly. After you leave rehearsal, the director will still be there. And they are the one who has to do all the heavy lifting and you shouldn't make it harder for them to get things done. So it's really important to make a good choice about who you work with. Sometimes the director is chosen for you and you have to work with who you have. Hopefully they are smart and will listen to you about your play. If not, don't work with them again. When I meet with a director for coffee to figure out if we work well together, I ask myself: Are they smart? Do they like the play? Do they understand the play? Will they listen to me? Are they a good director? If so, great! If not, it won't work. But there's only so much you can learn from meeting someone for coffee. Talk to other people they've worked with. What are they like to collaborate with? What does your gut say?

I like to go to rehearsals at the beginning and end of the process. I like to be there to answer questions at the first read-through and help get them started on the world of the play. I don't love to be around the whole time. Some writers do, but I think it helps me maintain an outside perspective and not get used to how they're actually doing it. I may come once in the second week if I can, but mostly I want to be sure to be around the last week—not for tech, unless I have to, but for run-throughs, to see what needs tweaking and adjusting.

With a new play, it's useful to be around to help with small rewrites. Big rewrites are hard for everyone, so try as much as you can to get the play in the best shape you can before rehearsals start. Sometimes an actor will have trouble with a scene or a line and they may look to you to fix it. Is it just that actor who is having the problem, or will everyone who plays this part have trouble? You may decide to let them work it out or you may decide you know how to make a fix to make sure this isn't always a problem with the play.

The danger is the temptation to change things that don't need changing to make actors happy. If it's to improve the play, yes, definitely make the change, but if it doesn't make the play better or even makes the play worse, you don't want to do that.

You have the right to be in rehearsals, but you may not always want to be there. It's not always fun to watch actors figure stuff out. But don't let anyone tell you that you aren't allowed in rehearsal. You are always allowed in rehearsal. No one can change your words without your permission. No one can add things or subtract things or move things around unless you say they can. You own your play. And all those rights should be in the contract you sign with the producer. The Dramatists Guild has standard contracts you can use and a "Bill of Rights" that clearly states what you're entitled to as a playwright. Read these documents. Know the rules and norms. Don't let anyone take advantage of you.

Sometimes a director will be leading the play in the wrong direction and you will have to fight for your play. This has not happened to me a lot, but it does happen. Speak up. Be polite but firm. Try not to hurt relationships. But fight for your work.

At the end of the day, you want the play to be as much of what you imagine it to be as possible. In many cases, actors and directors can make things better than what's on the page. They can be funnier and more poignant. These are the people you want to work with—those that make your work better. If they misunderstand the tone or the play, try very hard to get them back on track. You want to be judged for what you intended. It's very easy to be swayed by someone else's aesthetic. But make the work you want to make, not the work someone else wants to make.

And know that no perfect production exists. You can only hope the play will come through. Sometimes I see multiple productions of the same play and some actor in some college will be funnier than I've ever seen anyone do that part. Or there's an amazing set in another production. A moment works better than it ever has before. In my mind, sometimes, I want to take the set from this production and the actor from that production. But no ideal version will ever exist. We live in the reality of the live performance and we celebrate it.

But back to working with others: Be open to the ways things can work that were not the way you intended as long as the play still works. Make friends. Give compliments. Enjoy it when the play sings. But also argue for the moments you need. Before you burn a bridge, make very sure it's one you can afford to burn. Try very hard to stay on good terms with actors and directors. The theater is a very small world and people talk. Don't be the jerk no one wants to work with, but do stand up for yourself when you have to.

HOW PEOPLE REALLY TALK
AND ADAPTING THAT
FOR THE STAGE

It's really important to learn how to write good dialogue if you want to be a playwright. I guess that's kind of obvious. But what is good dialogue? Well, look, that's up to you. There is poetic dialogue and naturalistic dialogue. There are lots of different kinds of good TV dialogue, some of which I would consider bad in a play. Aaron Sorkin's dialogue in *The West Wing* is really different from Amy Sherman-Palladino's dialogue in *Gilmore Girls*. But they are both really compelling. Beckett's dialogue is really different from Tennessee Williams's. Find what kind you are drawn to. I think what's helpful is really listening carefully to how people around you actually talk. Then modify that for your own purposes.

Write down conversations you overhear as often as you can. Sit yourself on a bench or in a coffee shop for the express purpose of listening to how people talk. Write it all down in a notebook. As much as you can, remember the exact way someone says something.

When you turn realistic dialogue into play dialogue, adjustments sometimes have to be made so that your audience can understand what's happening. The trick is to make it sound real without it being boring and without it feeling written. In real life, people frequently don't speak in complete sentences. They leave important context out. People use different words than they mean to. People repeat themselves and interrupt themselves. They think they have said things they haven't said. The way people talk says a lot about where they grew up and who they interact with now. Lots of people have their own personal verbal tics. Most things real people say are not interesting in a theatrical context, but pay very close attention to when your ears perk up. Because people will also say the most amazing things.

Whenever I ask a class to bring in overheard conversations, I always think they won't be interesting enough, but they are always amazing. Whole worlds exist in a few lines. If you teach, have your students do this. Either way, start writing down what people say. I'm telling you. It will change the way you see and hear the world.

And it will help you write dialogue better.

Kelly Stuart, one of my professors, had us bring in found dialogue every week. I found it revelatory to see what different people brought in and what that said about them and about the world they inhabit.

Like I said, there are a lot of different styles of dialogue and part of finding out your writing style is figuring out what your specific characters sound like. Do they talk in paragraphs? Or one-word sentences? Are they effortlessly clever? Are they crude or polite or cryptic? Do they talk around the topic or are they blunt?

When you're starting out, I would suggest having people in your plays talk in a way that matches where you come from. The rhythms you grew up with are probably easier to write at a speed that will help you find flow in your writing session. Finding the flow regularly is very helpful for sustaining a career, so whatever you can do to find that for yourself, by all means do it.

My teacher Theresa Rebeck stressed upon our class the importance of having your characters sound different from each other.

This is especially helpful if you eventually want to write for TV. This is not a priority for my plays, and doesn't come naturally to me. But it's a helpful skill, so if you can do it, you should do it. The trick is to also make it sound real or consistent with the world you're making.

TIPS FOR WRITING
ACTIVE DIALOGUE

Avoid dialogue that's question, answer, question, answer.

IONESCO
What do you want?

BECKETT
I want to be happy.

IONESCO
Why do you want that?

BECKETT
I just do.

The questions and answers get really boring really fast. I see this pattern a lot in the work of early-career playwrights. Unanswered questions help create tension as long as you don't overuse them. My characters often talk past each other, sometimes don't listen, don't answer the question that's being asked. That's what I like to do. It doesn't mean that's what you have to do. What are your characters doing and how can you help them be more active? Marsha Norman says a good way to get exposition across is to have characters argue about it.

Another mistake I see sometimes: If there is more than one question, most humans answer the most recent question first.

NEIL
What are you doing here? Is that for me?

SUE
Yeah, if you want it.

Usually this doesn't happen in real life:

NEIL
What are you doing here? Is that for me?

SUE
I'm just hanging out.

Avoid things that take the tension out of your scene. In many of my first drafts, characters in say "I'm sorry" a lot, which can drain the tension. They say "I love you" a lot, too. I have to go in and find the moments that the characters are reducing tension and cut those parts. The whole goal is to keep the dialogue active and alive and surprising. Let your characters surprise you with things they say. If you decide later that you don't think they would say that, you can always change it.

When you're first starting, it may be difficult to tell if your dialogue is active or not without hearing it out loud. Are the characters trying to do things? Is there subtext—things they aren't saying which makes it feel like there's more going on underneath the scene?

Usually, young writers overwrite a lot. Characters repeat themselves a lot. I use repetition in my writing on purpose, but I have to be careful to do it in such a way that it's not overused. That will bore your audience. After your first draft is written, go in and see what you can delete without undermining the structure or meaning of the scene. My first drafts are always overwritten in some parts and underwritten in others. Hearing them out loud helps me identify those parts and fix them. No matter how much cutting I've done, once I'm in rehearsal for production, there will always be more cuts to make.

Monologues should be in the present tense. As much as possible, the story a character is telling feels more alive when you switch to present tense. This is something Tanya Barfield said to me once and it made a huge difference in my writing. Plays happen in the present moment. When you switch to past tense, you're putting up an extra wall, keeping the audience from properly engaging.

In the same way, it's helpful to dramatize an event instead of having a character tell us something that happened to them. Show, don't tell. Let us see it instead of telling us about something we wish we could have seen. Can the thing you're having your character describe be a scene we see instead?

Also, make sure the characters in the scene are who the scene is about. Don't have two characters talking about a third character who isn't there. Sometimes you have to do this, but know that each time you do that, it's not as dramatic as it could be. If the drama is offstage, you're making a less interesting, less exciting play. The dramatic action, the issues and problems of the play or of the scene should be between the people actually in the scene. If it's not, change your scene.

More than anything, you really don't want to bore your audience.

MISCELLANEOUS WRITING ADVICE POSED AS QUESTIONS THAT SOMETIMES APPLY TO YOUR PLAY

Are the stakes high enough for us to worry about or care about what happens next? So many times I'm reading a play by an early-career writer and I wonder why I'm reading it. I ask myself why I should keep going. You really want to hook your audience in the first five minutes with the main conflict or question of the play. Am I still watching because I need to know what will happen? Am I invested in these characters? Maybe I really like them or maybe I'm fascinated by them. Am I invested in the world of the play? Am I invested in what the play is trying to talk about? Do I want to know more about that topic, and does it seem like the writer is in a position to tell me more? Do I trust the hand at the wheel enough to want to go on this ride?

Why here, why now? In other words, why are the events of the play happening at this particular time? What are the circumstances that explain why this thing occurred today? Usually, this question is looking for a missing cause and effect. The play *Three Sisters* opens a year after the sisters' father died, and Chekhov chose that day for a reason. It adds tension to everything he sets up. It would be a different play if it was a day after their father died or if it was five years later.

What does the main character want? If someone asks you this about your play, it usually means "I don't know what your main character wants" or "I lose track of this during the play."

Why did you write this play? This is a question people don't usually ask directly but is sometimes the subtext behind other questions. Sometimes this gets at a feeling that the play isn't about enough. Or it's asking why we should be invested. Or it's asking if you're invested enough in the play you're writing. Or someone is looking at you and is confused about how you wrote this play. Sometimes it means that something isn't working, and they're confused about what you're trying to accomplish.

TAKE THE INITIATIVE AND ASK QUESTIONS

After teaching a class or visiting someone else's class, I used to tell students that they could email me with any additional questions. Very rarely did this ever happen. But I know many student playwrights have questions. Why didn't they email me when I told them they could? I think that if you (yes, you!) do take the initiative in that way or in whatever way you choose, you are rare indeed. Dare to do small things that other people don't do. Cold-email someone. Write a physical letter. Show up. Just showing up sometimes is the thing that makes a difference.

I have had coffee with so many young writers just because they emailed and asked me. And I think I was able to help many of them. For example, I have had many conversations with writers about publishers—I'm someone who works with a lot of publishers and can give the lowdown. But I only can do this for people who reach out. I'm not saying you should reach out to me. I will quickly get overwhelmed by the five people who will read this book and do that. But also, I'm not saying don't reach out to me. People who dare to send friendly emails often get friendly responses. And making a habit of this will build you a community of sorts. Make a habit of making friends. Make a habit of taking the initiative.

More times than I can tell you, at a writing retreat or panel, I find I'm the only one who knows who else will be there and what to expect. So many people just don't ask questions. Maybe they don't want to know or are too busy to find out. But if you want to know, ask questions. Sometimes it's the only way to find out what's happening. If you're thinking of working with a director or actor, email people they have worked with before. Do your research. Find out if there were any red flags or issues. Find out what you can about organizations and people. It doesn't take a lot of effort and theater people are mostly happy to help.

Also, figure out a way you can do things that other people wouldn't, using your own strengths and interests. I'll give you two examples. One, I had a blog back when people had blogs. I was in the third wave of theater blogs in the early 2000s and we were all talking theater and commenting on each other's blog posts. It was all about New York theater. But then my wife and I moved to Minneapolis for her Jerome Fellowship in 2008 and I couldn't post about New York theater anymore. I was trying to decide if I should shut down the blog or pivot to something else.

I was in New York for a couple of weeks in rehearsal for my play *Pretty Theft,* and we had some interest from press before opening. I was asked to do a couple of interviews and I really enjoyed it, and I thought other people might like to be interviewed, too. So I had the idea to use my blog to interview my friends who were playwrights. I had been in a lot of writing groups and knew lots of other writers, but I was also the kind of person who would find the one playwright at the party and spend the whole night talking to them. So I already knew lots of writers. I emailed them questions and they emailed answers back. I thought I would stop at fifty. I did it for about ten years and interviewed over 1,100 playwrights. And for a long time, I was known for my interviews much more than I was known for my plays. Sometimes if I went to a theater party with some younger playwrights in attendance, I was treated as if I was a celebrity, and as time went on, I lost count of whether or not I had interviewed people so sometimes I didn't know if someone was being nice to me because I interviewed them or because I had not yet asked them if I could interview them. In any case, the blog was a worthwhile use of my time. It created a community of sorts and it was helpful to some of the playwrights who weren't yet as well known. It made me more well-known and it was a way to help others. Did it help my career? Who can say? It definitely made my name more known in many theater circles and literary offices. It didn't hurt.

Another thing I did that probably still helps my career: most of my plays have monologues in them. This is partially because when I was learning to write plays, Kelly Stuart, one of my teachers, would sometimes have us stop a scene and, as an exercise, write a monologue to better get that character's perspective. That became part of my process and then part of my playwriting. Monologues just started sprouting up in my plays all over the place. And as my work evolved, the monologues remained a big part of my writing. Which is to say, most of my plays have monologues in them, in some cases quite a few. And I have a lot of published plays. I realized one way to get my work out there more was to put my monologues online. I put them on my blog first, and then I found other places online that housed monologues and emailed them and got my monologues on other sites. Because of that, I have over a hundred monologues online right now from thirty-something plays.

And it not only gets my name out there in the theater world, but I sell a lot more books because actors are told to read the play a monologue is from in order to understand how to do it well. Because I did this, I get a lot of messages from friends telling me they've seen three or four of my monologues at auditions, or young actors email to tell me they got into theater schools with my monologues. Like my blog, it's a thing that got my name out into the world. I have quite a few productions every year, but I think I'm more well known than I should be because of my monologues and because of my blog.

Those are two things that I did that helped my career that weren't writing plays and submitting plays. Do you have something like that? What can you do? What does your community need?

SPEAKING OF MY BLOG

You should totally read the interviews on my blog, by the way: aszym.blogspot.com. At one point, I was going to try to publish them all, but I realized the book would be at least 3,000 pages long and that was way too long. But I promise you—someone's interview will speak to you and your situation, whatever it is. I think I did a good job of interviewing a large variety of writers before I got tired and burned out and stopped doing it.

Nowadays, there are lots of excellent podcasts where you can hear playwrights talking about writing. Brian James Polak has a great one housed at *American Theatre* called "The Subtext." I love doing podcasts but I don't really listen to them; I prefer reading. Maybe that's why this is a book and not a podcast. And it's also why I liked posting the interview texts from playwrights.

I can't tell you how many times my mood was lifted and I was inspired by the interview answers some amazing writer emailed to me. And I got to read it first, before sharing it with the world. I always told them they could ignore questions they didn't want to answer or add questions they did want to answer. And I always asked, "What advice would you give to playwrights starting out?" Definitely take a look at some answers to that question—especially if they're from one of your theater heroes. I got to interview many of my own heroes.

People ask me what I learned from interviewing 1,100 playwrights. I knew there were a lot of us, but I think actually getting to talk to so many super-smart, super-talented people really put in perspective what an exciting time it is to be a theater artist. There are a lot of phenomenal, dedicated people doing the thing that we're doing. It can't be overstated.

And every year, new playwrights rise up or graduate from the many, many MFA programs. I've seen people stop writing plays. I've seen playwrights pass away. But more arrive every day, hungry and sharp and passionate.

Again, if you think of them as your competition, that can feel overwhelming. I try to think of them all as friends, even those I don't know yet or those I once knew who I haven't seen in ten years. You can be mad at the theater world. But don't get mad at the playwrights. We're all just out there trying to do the thing.

ON WRITING MONOLOGUES

Actors always want monologues for auditions and for classes. I know that many of the monologues from my plays are in circulation in these rooms. Now, for some things, students need monologues from published plays. But for a lot of things, they don't need that. They just want something good. You can write good monologues for your actor friend or for yourself if you are an actor.

Here are some tips, cribbed from the back of my monologue book from Applause, *Small Explosions*. Some of this advice applies to longer works, too.

1. First of all, you need a character who wants something from the person they are speaking to (besides a part in a play). So what do they want? Remember: the stakes should be high. Eternal love is a bigger want than a pencil. What are the different tactics your character can use to get what they want within one to two minutes?

2. Write about what you're interested in. But then make it personal. The character is more interesting than the information. Make sure we know how it relates to us as humans.

   Example: ". . . Which is why triceratopses have three horns. But you know what dinosaurs don't have? My fear of abandonment."

3. Play to opposites. Put the reversal or surprise right in the monologue. Add a twist. I do this a lot in my monologues. It often takes a turn at the end.

   Example: "And now that I've told you all the things that are amazing about you, [REVERSAL!] maybe I won't kill you after all."

   Do you change your mind over the course of the monologue? That's a good reversal and a way to create dramatic action. Start out trying to convince your audience of one thing and end up convincing yourself of the other.

4. Surprise yourself! And you will probably surprise others too.

5. Lists! I love lists. Here are the many ways I deceive myself and others. Here are all the secrets I've never told. Here are the things that are most bothering me. Many of my monologues are lists.

   Suggested Assignment: Write a list of "all the reasons I love you" and have them all be negative things.

6. Find the drama. Write about jealousy or revenge or betrayal or fear. Find the most powerful emotion you have and use that. Find universal feelings we can all tap into while making them specific to your character.

7. Fictionalize it so you don't cause problems. Or don't. I'm not the boss of you. I'm just saying: try not to cause a lot of unnecessary drama in your life by telling your friend's secrets in your monologue.

So those are some ideas, some formulas. Write the part you want to play or the part you think you can't play but will try to play. Reveal truths. Make jokes. Break my heart. Or all of the above.

THE GIFT MENTALITY, AND TALKING ABOUT MONEY

Like I wrote at the beginning, I'm thinking of this book as a sort of gift. I can't actually expect that the amount of hours it will take to put all this down on paper will come back to me in any monetary way. So I'm doing this because I want to do this.

I also write plays because I want to write plays. I get paid for it, eventually, yes, when it works out, but that's never been the primary motivator for me and I guess I'm arguing it can't be the primary motivator for you either. It has to come from a place of love. Because being a playwright is hard and, really, why else would you do it unless it was because you love theater and you love the feeling of seeing your play work like it's supposed to? You have to love actors and love the audience and want to make something cool to share with the world. That isn't to say you love these things all the time. Theater and the world are frustrating and hard. But finding the hope to create a new thing is what it's all about.

And you have to write what you want to write. Entertain yourself. Write the thing you think should exist that doesn't yet exist. If you don't see yourself on stage, write that person. A funny thing happens sometimes for me that when I'm commissioned to write a play, suddenly I don't really want to write that play. Sometimes, it's harder to write something when someone is paying you to write it. It becomes a job. There is a freedom to writing exactly what you want to when you want to. No one can tell you what you can and can't do. You can do anything! Sometimes when writing I am the most free I can be.

But when someone does want to pay you for a play, you have to figure out how to write that, too.

It took me twenty-five years of writing plays to figure out how to make a sort of living at it. Once most writers have a hit (or, nowadays, sometimes before they have a hit), they go off to LA and write for TV and film because it's very hard to make a consistent living as a playwright and they get tired of their day jobs. And once in LA, some of them don't write plays anymore. Or they won't have time to write and market a new play for a very long time. But somehow, some of them are able to do both. No many, but some.

If you're not a playwright who writes for TV, or you are supported some other way, you have to have a day job. Some writers are professors or work at theaters or do something unrelated to theater for work. Part of continuing to write is finding the job that won't exhaust you mentally, will allow you time to write, and will maybe give you the flexibility to go out of town to work on a play. It's an added bonus if you can find work with health insurance and retirement. There is no retirement fund or health insurance for playwrights, and we all get older a lot faster than we think we will. If you can, figure out how to start saving for retirement as early as possible. At the very least, put some money every year into a Roth IRA. I wish I had done this a lot earlier in my life. I also wish I hadn't taken on so much debt from grad school. More on this later.

Right now, I am making a modest living from royalties off of productions of my plays. Mostly these are published plays. About half of the royalties are from high school productions. Most of the other half are from small professional, indie, or community theaters. I may have one or two TCG theater productions in a normal year. And I make a small amount from book sales. I also make a little by doing video or in-person appearances in classes, sometimes but not always because the class is doing a play of mine. Occasionally I do a little teaching. I also have commissions, on average maybe one every two years. I have been paid as little as $200 and as much as $15,000 for a full-length play. Some playwrights who aren't me make money from grants and awards. If you can figure out grants, it may be an easier path forward, but I could never figure that out as a significant part of my income.

See Todd London's book *Outrageous Fortune* for an in-depth look at how playwrights do and don't make money. I am in the minority right now, in that I'm consistently making income from play royalties.

WRITING FOR
DIFFERENT MARKETS

My two primary markets are small indie theaters and schools. I would separate those two further into small professional theaters and community theaters, on the one hand, and high schools and colleges on the other. Some of my plays can be done at all four types of venue and some done at only one or two. (There are other kinds of markets I'm not going to go into below such as TYA—Theater for Young Audiences—by which I mean theater performed by adults for children. Also: Touring musicals. Christian plays done in churches. Black gospel plays. Sketch comedy. Plays in other languages. And I'm sure many more. I just don't know those worlds. But again—there are so many ways to be a playwright.)

Off-Broadway (along with Broadway, of course) is the target of most playwrights, or else large regional theaters in which a play can have its premiere and get enough attention to have many other large productions afterward. There are only so many of these theaters, and they do not have many slots not taken by already famous people, so it is very hard to get a new play produced in an Off-Broadway or large LORT house. Agents may suggest holding out for a first production at one of these places and try to help you build up the excitement and momentum to get to them. If it works, that's awesome. And if the show goes well, that can lead to more productions of the play all over the country for a couple years. But most often it just doesn't work, and playwrights don't take the next step to get their play out there. (More on that later in "Submitting.")

The next step down includes smaller regional and professional theaters. Some of these theaters look for new work. By all means, target them too.

There's an overlap between the theaters above and indie and community theaters. Sometimes it's hard to say how to best describe which thing a theater is. Do you go by the number of seats or the contract its actors are working under? LORT, SPT, something else? Do you go by how good the productions are, how much the ticket prices are, or how much you as a playwright get paid? In the end, it's not really important.

What is important to think about is where the play you're writing belongs. Is it a Southern play that the regional theaters of the South will embrace? Is it a gritty Off-Broadway show? Is it a broad farce that community theaters will love? Or is it the kind of farce that is also appealing to Off-Broadway commercial producers? The kind of play that the established Off Broadway theaters like in this era is often too edgy to play in the suburbs. And it rarely makes it to high school productions. Of course, there are exceptions to everything. But once you've written your play, it's helpful to figure out what kind of theater it belongs in.

My early plays had a lot of four-letter words in them because that's how my characters talked, and I didn't think about it at all because they were plays for adults. I eventually figured out that there were large parts of the country where you just couldn't do plays with lots of cursing in them—which most high schools definitely won't allow, either.

About ten years ago I had a play of mine produced at a high school for the first time and I was really excited about that. High school is where I learned to love theater and I was thrilled that I could help kids also discover theater for the first time. But if I wanted to continue to be done at high schools, I had to change the way I wrote some of my plays.

My play *Clown Bar* is violent and ridiculous and full of cursing. Colleges and small theaters love it. It's been running for three years in Ankara in Turkish. It's been done several time in Vegas. It's not a play high schools or theaters with suburban subscribers will do. If all my plays were like that, I don't think I would be making a living right now.

My play *Kodachrome* is done at all sorts of small and medium size theaters throughout the country. It's done a lot at high schools and colleges. It's not at all like *Our Town*, but people compare it to *Our Town*. It's sweet and funny and sad and there is nothing particularly offensive in it. If all my plays were like this, I would probably be making more money than I am.

But, really, the secret is to have one big hit that keeps getting done in as many markets as possible. Musicals can sometimes do this. John Cariani's *Almost, Maine* is a really good play that continues to get done in small and midsize theaters and in hundreds of high schools. It was moderately successful Off-Broadway but became a regional hit by word of mouth. There isn't really another play that compares to *Almost, Maine* in terms of high success in multiple markets. And I'm willing to bet many people reading this book have never heard of this play, which has been a constant staple all over the country since about 2009.

Moneywise, a small professional theater pays royalties that come to around $2,000–$5,000 for a run. A larger LORT venue can pay $5,000–$20,000, depending on the number of seats. A lot of small indie theaters will do a play for two or three weeks, which translates into around $800–$1,200 dollars. A small community theater or high school that does maybe three performances—that's about $300. Sometimes a high school will do one performance. So you need a lot more productions from schools and community theaters to add up to the same amount of money. However, high schools represent a gigantic market. My guess is that in any given year there are as many playwrights making a living from the high school market as there are from large, fancy productions. The people who I know who are making a consistent living year after year are definitely doing so in the high school and amateur markets. (Most of these writers, but not all of them, have written a lot of plays.)

One note about colleges: I expended a lot of effort trying to reach out to colleges years ago to try to get productions. I don't recommend wasting your time doing that unless it's with people or places near you or with which you have a relationship. I get a lot of productions at colleges now, but it's not because I submit to them. They find my published plays. It is usually too hard to figure out who the decision-maker is at a college. So many theaters at that level are student-run, and every year those students graduate and new ones arrive so the people deciding what play to do changes every year. You could email professors, but usually that doesn't work as well as reaching out to high school teachers. Professors hop around from school to school a lot, or alternatively they have been there so long they already have their own approach to choosing plays. Some programs may want to do a Broadway hit or a classic and have no interest in new plays. Maybe they want their students to do the "important plays." This doesn't happen as much in high school, but in both places you're competing against Shakespeare, whose plays are all free. Shakespeare is great, but I like new plays, and high schools are always looking for new plays.

WRITING FOR HIGH SCHOOLS

Like I said above, high schools comprise a huge market. There are many more high schools doing plays every year than other theaters and they are always looking for new plays to do. There are 26,000 high schools in the US, and a lot of schools outside the US also do plays in English. And then there are middle schools.

During the pandemic, schools started doing plays again a lot sooner than most theaters, first over streaming video and then in person. If you had a play high schools liked, you were one of the only playwrights making money from royalties during the pandemic.

Every school has different needs but they have a lot in common. They want good plays and they want flexible plays. They don't want cursing or alcohol use. They probably don't want guns unless your play is specifically about that. They hate sex. Some schools don't like kissing. Some schools don't want queer content. This is a different situation than with young-adult books, which can be much more intense and explicit than school plays: once the kids are onstage doing it and the parents are watching, everyone is much less comfortable with the content. High schools aren't doing Sarah Kane. Some colleges are, however.

Recently, conservative high schools have gotten more conservative and progressive schools have gotten more progressive. So there is a big range in terms of what a high school may be looking for. As always, write the play you want to write, but understand your choices affect the size of your market.

High Schools want one-act plays (25–35 minutes) for competitions, and they want hour-long, 90-minute, or two-hour plays for regular productions. They want dramas and comedies. They like plays about teenagers but will do other things, too. Sketch comedy around a topic works well. So does issue-based drama. Adaptations are also popular, as are new takes on known characters. Play publishers already have all the Sherlock Holmes and Alice in Wonderland they need unless you have an exciting new take.

There are school competitions all over the country but the biggest market is in Texas. If you get a one-act that does well in competition in Texas, it will likely be done a lot the following year, and maybe for a while after that. Keep in mind that one-acts pay about half what full-lengths pay, but they're easier to write and are in demand.

You want plays that are flexible in terms of cast size and gender. Ideally your show can use 20–30 actors but can be done by fewer. Teachers love when most of the scenes are for two people. It's easy to rehearse. Keep sets and design elements simple, because school budgets are often very low.

If you want to write for high school, read a bunch of plays written for high school. Stage Partners and Playscripts let you read most or all of the play on their sites. Other publishers for high school and middle schools include Dramatic Publishing, Concord Theatricals/Samuel French, Youthplays, Heuer Publishing, Pioneer Drama Service, Eldridge Publishing, Big Dog Publishing, Brooklyn Publishers, Uproar Theatrics, and more. The main publishers that don't specialize in high school are also sometimes interested in plays that can be—but don't have to be—done in that market. Also check out the Educational Theatre Association's annual lists of most produced full-length and one-act plays in high schools.

There are a few Facebook groups where drama teachers talk about what they need and what they're looking for, and you can pitch your new and published plays there. "High School Theatre Directors and Teachers" allows playwrights to pitch a show on the first of every month. I have definitely gotten productions that way. If you are helpful in those groups and engage a lot on the Facebook pages without being annoying, often the effort is rewarded over time.

Like anything, research helps. You get out of it what you put into it.

Some drama teachers are hard-core theater people and some are doing it for the first time and don't know a lot. Musicals are huge. Known quantities are done a lot more than anything else. Right now, everyone is doing *Clue* and *The Addams Family* for example.

If you know a high school drama teacher, it's helpful to test your plays with their class. And it's a good way to get that first production that you usually need before getting a publisher interested. If you don't know teachers, get to know them. Figure out what works and doesn't work. What do teachers like? What do the students want to do? There is great variety all over the country in what schools are looking for, but there are trends you will begin to see quickly.

(Much of this I learned from Morgan Gould and Jason Pizzarello—who both used to work at Playscripts but now run Stage Partners—and from many conversations with Don Zolidis and a bunch of other playwrights, most recently Tracy Wells.)

One more thing I should say: I think some theater artists look down on writing for young people in the way folks used to look down on writing for TV. It's easy to be a snob in the theater world, and I know I've had my moments of snobbery. And, yes, there are a lot of bad plays written for students, and many high school students also do not yet have acting chops. So, yeah, it's not like working with your most talented friends. But it does take a lot of talent to write in such a way that even students who don't have a lot of skill will succeed in front of the audience. A friend of mine used to refer to this kind of writing as "actor-proof."

I'm not saying that you have to write for high schools. But I think introducing youth to good plays made for them is a worthy goal. Helping create the next generation of theater lovers is something worthwhile to spend your time doing, while giving you access to the most consistent market in which you can make money from writing plays.

MORE ON SNOBBERY

You don't need to pretend to like things you don't like, but try to be nice, and try not to knock down other people who are trying to do this thing. It is very hard to write a good play. It is harder still to have a good production. We're in this together, all trying to make art in whatever way we can.

When you label someone a loser for a failure or what you perceive as a failure, you hurt yourself as much as them. An artistic life is full of ups and downs. Next time the failure could be yours and you don't deserve to be called a loser any more than they do.

But also we learn from our mistakes, or we should try to. And some people with big egos who are not trying to become better artists are occasionally successful. But they should be pitied. It's easy to become bitter over bad art succeeding. But that only hurts you.

To be clear, I don't mean you shouldn't be exacting in your revisions and try for excellence in your work. Just don't be an asshole about it. Yeah?

I really can't stress enough what a bad idea it is to publicly trash someone else's work. Odds are you will want to work with someone involved in that play at some point and you don't want to get on their bad side. But, also, you don't want a bad reputation. You don't want to make enemies or put that bad karma into the world. By all means, you should discuss plays with your friends and be as brutal and honest as you can. It's helpful to figure out why things don't work and it's helpful in figuring out what kind of artist you are by knowing what kinds of work you don't want to make. Just don't do it publicly. Walk a couple blocks away from the theater before talking about a show you just saw. Don't be unkind online.

It's really easy to tear down someone else's art. It may feel good in the moment. But, really, you're just ingesting your own poison.

SAYING THANK YOU

I feel like a lot of persevering as a playwright involves not giving into bitterness. At least, it's something I struggled with. A counterintuitive thing that helps is being grateful for things that do come. No career can happen without a lot of help from a lot of people. If you have a play published, have a page where you thank people who helped the play or your career. Dedicate it to someone who you are grateful for. Probably no one besides me will tell you to do this. Lots of published plays don't have Dedication or Special Thanks pages because the playwright didn't think to put them in. I think it's a lost opportunity. I really love publicly thanking someone by dedicating a book to them and I think most of them are overjoyed at being thanked in this way, too. When my wife dedicated a play to me, I framed that page and put it in my office. It's still one of my most prized possessions.

Write thank-you cards for everyone involved in your premiere production and give them out opening night. Refer to the program so you don't forget anyone. This is time-consuming but important. I always start this process feeling like it's a drag and I don't have time for it, and I always end up in a good mood, happy I did it.

When you focus on what and who you're thankful for, you're not focusing on what you don't have and what you didn't get. There are going to be so many more things that you don't get every year, no matter how well things are going, and it's easy to just think about what isn't happening instead of looking at what is.

Send thank-you cards to people who have helped you in your career. Most literary roles in theater are thankless service jobs and those folks are never thanked or appreciated enough.

There is a lot of writing about the role of gratitude in being happy. And much of that advice is about thanking people and writing things down you're grateful for every day. And I get that sometimes it's hard to be grateful. But playwriting is a long-haul job, and to keep going, you can't succumb to hopelessness. Gratitude is one thing that helps you and your relationships with others.

CAST SIZE

The general wisdom is that small-cast plays are the easiest to get produced. And I agree. Mostly. A lot of theaters that do new plays can only afford four actors. A good two-character play is exactly what they want, especially for a second or third stage, which is where less-established playwrights are often relegated. After the pandemic, it seemed like there were so many more one-person shows happening than normal, and I think a big part of that was that there was less money for shows at a lot of theaters.

That said, the plays of mine that are done the most are flexible and can be done by small, large, or medium-size casts. Or they are done by large casts in ensemble-based or indie theaters. *Clown Bar* is an hour-long play with a cast of ten, and it has four songs. It is male-heavy. It's exactly what they told me not to do. But it has done pretty well and has even gone up at a couple larger theaters.

When I write new plays now, I mostly try to write more female characters than male characters or have a lot of characters that can be played by any gender. Most theater companies have a lot more talented women than men, and if you can write good parts for them, they may want to do your play.

If a theater really likes a play I don't think cast size matters as much as people think it does. Sarah DeLappe's *The Wolves* has a cast of ten and is done all over the country. (Although I bet a good number of theaters were permitted to use some non-Equity actors for many of the younger parts, which made it less expensive.)

CAST SIZE

Something that may make more of a difference than cast size to the potential number of future productions is whether you need a specific kind of actor who is hard to find in some communities. I recently read a really cool play about sumo wrestlers by Lisa Sanaye Dring, but I bet finding the six actors that play requires is difficult for a lot of theaters. But the play is really good and as of this writing, it has already premiered at a large regional theater and is about to have another production.

So yes, think about cast size, but also try to write a really good play. If you do, and you can get it in the right hands, sometimes productions will follow anyway.

GETTING THAT
FIRST PRODUCTION

Self-producing is a good idea, especially early on. I self-produced and directed a play of mine when I was in college. The easiest time to do it is when you're at school. There is free space and actors who want to do something. You don't have to pay for liability insurance or even work that hard to get people to come, and you probably don't have to charge admission. You need an audience for your play to know what works, and you might just get hooked the first time a room full of people laughs at something your character says.

So self-producing is a good way to get your first production of a play. Start a theater company and do your plays. Find a director you love, maybe a few actors you love, and figure out how to do all the things running a theater entails. There are many articles and a couple books about how to self-produce. But also talk to the people in your city who are already doing it. They already know what the good spaces are, and how the local fringe festival works if there is one in your area. Did they hire a PR person? Is that a thing you have to do? (In New York, I think it is.) Do you have to run for at least three weeks to get a reviewer to show up?

If you have your own theater company, you don't need anyone's permission to put up your own work. But you also have to do a lot of work to make the play happen. Producing is a whole other skill set with its own learning curve. Can you find a producer to work with?

The other way—which is the way I've done it the most—is to submit plays to lots and lots of theaters.

SUBMITTING

Don't submit a play before it's the best you can make it. How will you know this? You won't. But definitely hear it out loud, then revise, then hear it out loud again. Try to get rid of all the typos in the process. You should have at least one reading in front of an audience before you send it out into the world, in my opinion. You learn a lot by hearing an audience respond to the play.

Okay, so let's say you're happy with it and you suspect people will like it. (Or you hope so, anyway—the important thing is you think it's good and that a theater should do it. You don't have to feel this way every day, but you do have to want to get your work out there.) What's next?

The secret is that most playwrights don't send their plays to enough places. When I was a young playwright, Adam Bock said to me that you have to send your play to about 100 places. I took this to heart and every time I've done this, something has happened. For every 100 places you send a play, you're probably going to get one thing. If you get three things, that's awesome. Five is shockingly amazing. So, really, you have to figure out how to get as many people as possible to read your play. Even if it's the most amazing thing in the world—your masterwork—it's not going to be everyone's thing. Taste is subjective. Don't be surprised when you get very different responses from the same play. That's just how it goes.

So how do you find places to send your play? You need to be assertive but polite. First, send it to people you know. Ask politely if you may send it to actors who might be good in it, directors who would direct it well, theaters who do work that's like your work. And meet more people. Go see plays. Meet everybody and if you like their work, tell them. Don't send the play to people whose work you don't like. That may sound obvious, but maybe it isn't.

Send to the usual places—theaters who put out calls, places that specialize in development. The Dramatists Guild and Playwrights' Center have listings. NYCPlaywrights.org is great. There are online listings of places looking for things, and new development opportunities come up all the time.

Sometimes it's helpful to send a play to a development opportunity or contest even if you know your play is not exactly the kind of play they would choose. Literary people move around a lot and also talk to each other. If they read and like your play, they may tell someone else about it. They could recommend it to a theater that might program it. Or they could remember it when they move to another theater that might be a better match in a couple years.

But more than that, find the theaters your play will fit in. Scour the internet. Read a lot of plays. See a lot of plays and figure out whose plays are like your plays. Maybe get a smart theater person or two to help. Ask them, "Whose plays are like my plays?" Let's say you have a name or two or you have the names of a few plays. Now Google those names and make a list of theaters. What theaters are doing plays by the people who are like you? That's what you want to find out. This doesn't work if you're googling plays that were big Off-Broadway hits or just won the Pulitzer, because some theaters are just programming the most lauded new thing. So find the semi-famous plays like your play and lesser-known works by known writers who you write like. This is easier than you imagine once you identify what kind of a writer you are. On Concord's and Dramatists Play Service's sites, for example, they show where a play is currently being done. Playscripts shows every production a play has had.

Most of all, find theaters who are doing new plays—who will do a play that hasn't been done before or has only been done a couple times. All over the country there are small theaters doing new plays and basically every kind of play that exists can find a home. Whether you write like Tom Stoppard or Sarah Kane or Qui Nguyen or Brooke Berman or Jenny Schwartz or Mike Lew or Noah Haidle or Adam Rapp or Katori Hall, someone is looking for your play right now.

So, yes, find the online postings of new play submission opportunities and, yes, send to those places, too, but also approach the small theater in Minneapolis that seems like they would be into the thing you are doing. They get fewer submissions. There is a smaller pool your script will sit in, so your chances are better that the theater will actually produce your play—if it's the kind of play they do, that is. They are actively trying to find the perfect thing for their actors, their audience, their aesthetic. If you have that thing and it's good, you are helping them by reaching out.

How do you reach out? If they have guidelines on their site, follow the guidelines. If not, send an email. I'm probably fancier than you and I think it's more likely the person I'm emailing has heard of me. So you may not get as many responses as I do, but basically, I email the Artistic Director or Literary Manager or someone with "Artistic" or "New Works" in their title and say, "Hi! I think I have a play that fits with your theater's aesthetic. Can I send it to you?" Or, "Based on your past productions, I think I have a play you might like. Can I pass it along?" Something like that. But use your own words. And most of the time they will say yes.

Hit send. Then forget you sent it. Move on to the next thing. Sometimes it takes three years for someone to read something. Sometimes you will never hear from them again. This is a time-consuming process, but the more you learn what is out there and figure out what theaters are right for your plays, the easier it will become.

Send to the UK if you can, too, because British theaters tend to read plays and send rejection letters quickly. Not everyone has plays that are right for the UK and mostly they do plays by British writers, so pay attention to which American plays they do to see what might be right for those theaters.

So send to as many places as you can—near where you are, far away, wherever you can with whoever is there. Don't wait for the fancy theater to bite—by all means, send your plays there if you can, but don't wait. Get your play up now. If you have to produce it yourself, produce it yourself. The only way you will become a better playwright is by getting your plays on their feet in front of audiences.

Some theaters ask for a synopsis of your play. I want to stress the importance of brevity in both your synopsis and query letter. Fiction writers spend a lot of time on their query letters. We can learn from them. If their query is successful, it becomes the way for the agent who takes them on to sell the book and eventually a version of what they wrote in their query letter appears on the published book's jacket. You are marketing your play to whoever is reading your email, be it an Artistic Director or a Literary Intern. Try to give them a taste of what is exciting about your play without complimenting your own play. (No one will take you seriously if you tell them how great your play is, even if it's true.) If they like the play, they also have to market the play to get people to come see it. They may not see the way to do that if you don't help them in your description of your play.

Besides a longer synopsis, I would suggest you figure out a logline—that is, a one-sentence description that contains within it the essence of the play and also what is exciting to you about the play. A quick Google search of film loglines should help. Or read a bunch of entries on the New Play Exchange (NPX, newplayexchange.org) to see how peer playwrights market their plays. Go look at what is new from the play publishers. What piques your interest about a description? Notice the books you want to read or the films you want to see. What about their descriptions make you want to experience those works of art? How can you take what you learn from that back to your own work?

I don't particularly think I'm that good at describing my work, but I'm better than I used to be. You too can get better. Enlist a playwriting friend to help. Write each other's loglines.

Theater ebbs and flows. Theater companies are born, theaters shutter their doors. It's important to find the people who are doing exciting things right now that are like your thing. It's a lot of work to polish your synopsis and find places to send your play. But when you don't do that, your play sits on a shelf or on your hard drive and no one ever sees it except you. To have a career, you have to put yourself out there over and over and over again. And it gets easier in some ways as time goes on, but it's still just as hard in other ways.

When I was first starting out, I was printing and mailing scripts out to theaters. It was very expensive. Now that everyone just emails everything and computers have almost unlimited space for PDFs, it's a lot easier to send something somewhere—but it's also easier for a theater to never read your play or to get overwhelmed with scripts. The O'Neill gets 1,500 submissions some years. While I think it's still worthwhile to submit to the O'Neill, you'll have much better luck sending to a small theater that hasn't put out a call. They're probably reading less, and your script is more likely to get more attention or at least a read from someone who makes the decisions.

Yes, post your plays on New Play Exchange. It will not solve your career for you. Most of what it does is invisible. Fancy theaters are not choosing their seasons from plays they download from NPX, but if they read or hear about you they might look you up and if you don't have a website, or even if you do, they might want to have a taste of what you're up to if they have five minutes or thirty minutes. So it's helpful to have a presence there, to wave your flag around and maybe post an artist's statement. Or just put your plays up. I have gotten some school and small community productions from it, but I don't think most people get productions from it.

Even so, it's a tool and a large active database. Besides seeing what's out there, what it does is help in creating community. Read other people's plays, and if you like them, write recommendations for them and tell them you've done that so they know. Make friends with other writers, both online and in your community. Talk shop. Make friends. Writing is lonely. You don't have to be.

PUBLISHERS

Publishers are a mystery to a lot of playwrights. Most of the time you have to approach publishers and not the other way around.

Is your play ready to be published? Are you pretty much done rewriting it? Has it had at least one production that was reviewed? Do you have positive pull quotes and possibly some good production photos the publisher can use to market the play? If so, yes, submit your play to a publisher.

All of that goes for plays suitable for high schools, too, but a few publishers of plays for high schools don't require a production. (And if it's a play only for high schools, reviews don't matter, either.) However, if it hasn't been done yet, how do you know it works? Unless you've been doing it a long time, seeing the production is the thing you need to adjust and fix to help future productions succeed.

The two big publishers are Dramatists Play Service and Concord Theatricals (also known as Samuel French). Others are Playscripts (Broadway Licensing is comprised of the Playscripts and DPS imprints), Broadway Play Publishing, Theatrical Rights Worldwide, Original Works Publishing, Dramatic Publishing, and Next Stage. Applause is starting to publish new plays.

The British have different publishers, like Nick Hern and Oberon. (In the UK they do this cool thing where you can buy the published playscript of the new play you're seeing in the lobby at the theater. Lots of people buy the play they're seeing that night.)

I'm sure there are some publishers I'm forgetting. And musicals have different licensors and publishers. Go to Drama Book Shop in New York and see who publishes your favorite plays.

The two biggest publishers have a huge catalog. Concord has 12,000 titles. By contrast, Broadway Play Publishing has 1,200—including *Angels in America*, by the way. So if you have a choice of publisher, know that it's possible to languish in a smaller house or in a bigger house. It's easier for a smaller publisher to market everything they have, but a bigger publisher may have a more extensive email list. You could get lost in a big catalog or you could get more attention there than in a smaller catalog. It all depends how they market you, timing, luck, and so on. And so much can happen, too, from word of mouth. All publishers have different levels of reach, but they can all get things out into the world more than you can on your own. (Which doesn't mean you should stop showing it to people and submitting it once it's published.) Publishers also get plays in libraries, but some publishers are a lot better at that than others. You can search on WorldCat or your local library to see what plays are and aren't there. You can also donate your published plays to your local library.

It's a great feeling, the first time you hold your published play in your hand. You open the box up and there it is—your play with your name on it. People can buy it and read it and you don't have to have send it to them. It's great! Enjoy this! I urge you to enjoy your successes as much as you can. If you're not enjoying the good things about being a playwright—if seeing your play work in front of people or when you get fan email or when someone tells you they want to do your play doesn't make you at least a little happy every time—it will be harder to weather the hard times and the silences.

Note: I can't really recommend self-publishing unless you have a working method of driving traffic to your publications. I think the market is just too small without the help of a publisher. This is too bad, because self-publishing is easier than ever and it's possible to make professional-looking books with a little bit of effort. If you successfully figure out how to have to have a large reach, you can publish and license from your own website, but I think for most of us, that's not a viable method. Likewise, if you're someone who does a lot of events, you could self-publish and sell books after the show like you're a rock star. For years I've been trying to do what the British theaters or Playwrights Horizons do and sell books at the premieres of my new plays. If you can figure out how to do that, again, I don't think it's a money-making scheme, but it's so, so cool. Too often I'm revising up until the production and there's no time to figure out how to publish a book before it opens.

Once the play is published, you can relax, right? Kind of. Maybe you have a little help you didn't have before. But you should continue to tell theaters and people about that play. Continue to talk about when the play is having productions in person and online, if you do social media.

Think about how you can leverage your successes into more success. When I first had a play published, I sent out actual letters to theaters. Back then, you would still do that. I don't know if it helped at all. I also emailed theaters I found online that I thought would like my newly published plays. I said something like, "My play _____ has just been published by _____ and I think you would like it. Can I send it to you?"

A cold email like this led to a relationship at a midsize theater that has been one of my theatrical homes for the last twelve years. I don't know how many other emails I sent that led nowhere or that led to something else years later. But you have to try stuff.

LEVERAGE

The idea of promoting yourself and using success to try to get more success is really obvious and comes naturally to some people, but it's a new idea for others. It's about attempting to leverage what you have to get to a new place. Sometimes that just means talking about success, which is hard for some people. If you use social media, tell people when readings and productions happen. Or else, or also, have an email list that people can opt out of if they wish.

Theater people often will help each other out—I've gotten so many opportunities from other playwrights. But if they don't know about your play, they won't know it's exactly what their friend is looking for. So you have to talk about it. But it also can't be all you talk about, or you will become the annoying person everyone tunes out. And you should promote your friends, too, and tell people about their work.

When you have a public reading, tell theaters, directors, and producers who you think would like the play. Even if they're far away, tell them about it in case they want to read the play. When you have a production, tell people about it while it's happening. Post photos and videos. Productions lead to more productions only when enough people know about them. When they see the photos or read pull quotes from reviews, they might get interested and want to do it in their own community. Early on, so much feels like it's about building momentum to get enough excitement from enough people to get that first or second production of the play. And most of the time it doesn't work. But you have to keep at it in a way that doesn't overwhelm everyone you know but is also enough to have an effect. It's a tricky tightrope to walk, but it's kind of what has to happen.

You have to keep at it. Over and over again. Pretty much all the time. And it moves in cycles and changes as doors close or open, as people move from one job to another, as theaters close and new ones open, as new artists come on the scene.

The late Jim Houghton, an inspirational arts leader who created the Signature Theater in New York, among other things, used to say, "Go through the door that's open. Not the door you want to be open."

In other words, work with the folks in front of you. Find the people drawn to your art and make art with them. By all means knock on every door you can, but know you can only go through the doors that open. And those doors are different for everyone. We have no control over who will respond to our art. That doesn't mean you should make art with artists you don't respect. Make good things with good people, and work hard to find those people. But if you knock on the door of the fancy theater and it doesn't open, don't give up on your art. Find a way to get your play out there in other ways. I never intended to write plays for high school, and now it's a big and fulfilling part of my artistic life.

There's no way of knowing where your path will lead. Will it lead to short films or audio dramas or video game scripts, TV, feature films? There's no way to know until you put yourself out there. But you don't have to do anything you don't want to. If you love plays, write plays. That's what I've been doing almost exclusively for twenty-five years. And I got to go to some really cool places and had some amazing actors work on my stuff.

PIVOTING/FLEXIBILITY

Pivot from what isn't working. The pandemic was a big time for pivoting. All theater just stopped, though some continued soon after over streaming video and some fast writers wrote Zoom plays. I wrote a play for a parking lot that people could watch from their cars or lawn chairs. It had about four productions but I think the people who figured out how to write Zoom plays did a lot better.

Sometimes it takes a while to figure out if a play of yours is a success or not. It takes a while, sometimes, just to get that first production. But if you're getting a lot of positive responses you may want to further explore the kind of play that did well for you. Likewise, there may be plays that are less successful and you may not want to write more in that vein. I wrote sequels of a couple of my most-produced plays, thinking that the people who loved those worlds might want opportunities to live in them for longer. Then the pandemic happened and no one wanted nine- or ten-character plays. They are just starting to be done now in slightly larger numbers. In a few more years I may be able to tell you if writing these sequels was worth it monetarily or not. I can tell you now they were fun to write and I don't regret the time I spent on them.

How can you do more of what you do best in your writing but at the same time not bore yourself by repeating too much? I was impressed when I discovered Chuck Mee had three plays that used the same monologue. Very few people will read all our work or pay much attention. Feel free to steal from your own plays if you want. You have a moment that works? Do it in the next play. If you want. I mostly do that accidentally. So many of my plays have graveyards in them. There are lines of dialogue I have discovered in multiple plays of mine. No one cares. No one pays that much attention. So lean into the purest form of what you want to do. Do it again if it went well. Pivot away if you're bored with your own bullshit or if it didn't work.

Besides pivoting in your writing, again find the way to do what other people aren't doing. Some people make the most of new technologies, figuring out how to game the system or the algorithms. What are you good at? Or what can you figure out how to do? How can the skills you already have or are willing to develop help you in your life and in your art?

TALKING TO DONORS

Sometimes you will be asked to meet with, have dinner with, or stay with donors. I have had lots of luck meeting a lot of great people who love theater. Some donors I've met know more about theater and see more plays than I do. But more often you field a lot of questions from folks who don't understand a lot about what playwriting entails. This can be exhausting, especially if you're not expecting it or if you just got off a plane. Or if you are extremely introverted. One thing you may end up doing more than a few times is having dinner with wealthy people who support the arts, or with lawyers, doctors, or engineers who were frugal in life and are generous with theaters.

One piece of advice that I often was unable to take: Don't tell wealthy people how poor you are. It makes them uncomfortable and helps no one. For some reason I would get one drink in me and I would be talking about how expensive it is to live in New York. I'll also caution you not to drink too much. If you can drink in moderation, do. If not, don't drink. You don't want to be sloppy drunk around people who the theater you're at depends on. There are many times I've said the wrong thing sober, but saying the wrong thing is even more likely after a couple of drinks.

But, also, forgive yourself when you mess up. Apologize to others if you owe them apologies and move on. Theater is so much about relationships, and having good relationships with theater arts workers and donors and board members is helpful. So try.

But also know that if you're awkward, you're not alone. Most playwrights are.

Tell them how much you like the theater. Charm them if you can. If you can't, it's okay. But occasionally, a wealthy donor will champion your play and might even give money to a theater to make your play happen. So getting along well with donors is helpful sometimes for you directly or more often for the theater you're visiting.

The main audience and funders of American theater are older white people, so as a playwright, you will come in contact with them regularly at talkbacks and parties and opening nights. Figure out your strategies for moving in that world. This is especially hard for those of us who have never been around the very wealthy. But being a playwright and talking to people outside the professional theater world often involves explaining the same things over and over. So you'll have lots of practice. And, usually, they're excited to meet an artist. Stay curious. You can meet a lot of interesting people with very different lives than you sometimes. That's always helpful for a writer.

And know that if something isn't right or you get a bad feeling, absolutely get out of there. You are doing the theater a favor, and not the other way around. No donor conversation is worth harm to your mental health or safety.

Which brings me to talkbacks.

TALKBACKS

Talkbacks after a reading are primarily for the theater and to a lesser extent for you. For them, it's helpful to get their audience engaged. I avoid talkbacks if I possibly can. Sometimes it's helpful to answer questions about your play and hear from the audience at a reading, but mostly I find them not very helpful and occasionally destructive.

One thing that can happen is that folks who were enjoying a play in a reading will start to take the play apart in a talkback, and it will change the way they feel about the play. They can be convinced by others about flaws that may or may not be there. Or they will casually attack the play in devastating ways. This doesn't happen a lot, but I've seen it enough that I feel like I should mention it.

It's useful if the moderator knows how to shut down unhelpful people or if they frame the talkback in such a way to only allow for certain kind of questions or comments. I suggest you have a phrase in your back pocket to pre-empt comments that might be harmful and also use the talkback to ask questions of the audience. Sometimes a simple "Thank you, I understand" will stop someone from continuing.

Always ask for compliments. What was their favorite part of the play? What do they remember most? People want to talk about themselves and how to play relates to their lives. If you're trying to run out the clock and get out of there, you may ask them to do that.

I was at the JAW New Play Festival in Portland, Oregon with Jen Silverman, and she blew my mind when an audience member asked her a question at her talkback and she responded, "What do you think?" It never occurred to me to do that. For that reason only, go to other playwrights' talkbacks. You can learn some methods other writers use to navigate them. You might figure out your new favorite phrase to tactfully handle a difficult audience member.

NOTES ON YOUR PLAY

You will get a lot of thoughts on your plays. Sometimes you will ask for them and sometimes they will be given to you even though you don't want them. Definitely follow the golden rule and make sure to be non-prescriptive when giving feedback on other people's work—that is, don't tell them how you would write their play. And answer the questions they ask and only those questions. Don't give them notes if they don't want notes. The most helpful things are usually telling people the experience you had watching or reading the play. Where were you very engaged? When did you find yourself less engaged? Were you confused at all? You can say, "I thought this was happening. Is that what you wanted me to think?" Don't tell them how to rewrite it. Always start with something positive. If you don't do that, it can make it hard for them to listen to what you have to say. Let them know you're on their side, but also really be on their side.

Sometimes people ask questions to show that something was unclear. They may say, "What did the main character want?" and so you answer that question in the moment, but sometimes what they really mean is, "I didn't know what the main character wanted." So look for notes disguised as questions.

Sometimes when you get the same note over and over, that might be something to look at. Make sure the play is doing the thing you want it to do and is not accidentally saying the opposite of what you intend. Trust your gut on which notes to listen to and which to ignore. Make sure that, in thinking about revisions, you are writing toward what the play wants to be and not away from it. People can be very persuasive about what they think a play should be. Sometimes, the more persuasive they are, the more excited they are about what the play is about. That doesn't mean they are right. Very smart people can give you notes that are very smart but wrong for your play.

Sometimes there is a power imbalance and you're getting notes on a play from the Artistic Director of a theater. If you possibly can, ask them if it's a play they're considering for their season or not. If they aren't, there is no point in considering any notes you aren't sure about. Most of the time they're trying to help you make your play better, but everything they say carries a lot of weight and you might be convinced because you may think they know what works and doesn't work. And sometimes they do. But rewriting your play to their specifications in the hope they will produce it rarely works, in my experience. Unless they explicitly say it's a play they are interested in, you should not assume it's a play they are interested in.

When you get notes from actors, know that living in the play, even for a reading, can give them a perspective that's very helpful for a playwright. They may see problems you can't, and so you should listen to them carefully. But, sometimes, if they say they don't think the character would do that, what they mean is that they wouldn't do that themselves. Also, they may think their character should do more and be more. Sometimes they are right but sometimes they are not. I try to write parts that people want to play and try not to write thankless roles, but sometimes what the play needs is different than what an actor needs.

It takes practice to listen to notes and pick out what's helpful from what's not helpful. People who don't like the play occasionally may have something helpful to say, but they often don't. If they don't understand what you're doing or don't like what you're doing, their notes may not be helpful. Sometimes you will get someone who is casually cruel or intentionally destructive about other people's work who will make you feel like your play is terrible.

Sometimes you will get a bunch of notes and be excited about rewriting, and other times you will feel like shit and have no idea what to do. There are some teachers who have destroyed playwrights with notes and made them not want to write again for many years. I hope you don't run into these people. But if you do, you need to have your self-worth and your art survive the experience. Sometimes a teacher will save the harsher notes for someone who seems like they can take it. Sometimes they are wrong. I know quite a few people who had to rediscover their voice after grad school. I know of some famous, well-regarded playwrights who made a habit of tearing apart the work of younger writers.

Don't try to tear anyone down. The harm will come back at you. The theater world is small, and the word gets around about assholes.

HOW TO COME BACK
FROM DESTRUCTIVE NOTES

Sometimes, something said in a talkback or a notes session will knock you down for a while. I know several playwrights who couldn't go back to a play for years after a bad notes session. Some stopped writing altogether for years. I hope this doesn't happen to you. I hope someone won't make you lose your voice or your confidence. Sometimes this happens even when a note is meant to be helpful.

How do you bounce back from this? It may be the same way you bounce back from rejection or from heartbreak. Everyone has different methods. Do the thing that works for you. Sad music on repeat. Burning effigies. Witchcraft. Scheduling a massage. Whatever.

Please remember it's your play and no one else can tell you how to write or rewrite it. No one really knows anything when it comes to what will succeed in the world. You deserve to make your art how you want. So revise it or don't revise it, or write the next thing. Don't let yourself be broken. I'm well aware that bouncing back is much easier for some people than others. But it's a skill you will have to learn in this business. A very successful TV show creator and playwright posted online recently how a small theater reached out wanting to collaborate; he responded, and they proceeded to ghost him. Theater can humble you at all levels of your career, and no amount of success will completely protect you. Don't read Goodreads. Don't read the comments. If you're the kind of person who can't handle a bad review, don't read your reviews. Christopher Durang never read his reviews and he was a genius.

HAVE A WRITING GROUP

Figure out a way to have a writing group full of supportive people that you trust. This may take a while to find. Apply to writing groups that some theaters run. If necessary, create one yourself. Meet at someone's house or over Zoom, once a week or once every two weeks or once a month. You can either each bring pages to read aloud—usually ten or twenty minutes of a play—or you can bring an entire play to read and talk about. Sometimes it's helpful just to hear it out loud. If you have some amazing writers who are also supportive people, it's helpful to get constructive notes afterward, too.

I have been in so many writing groups over the years. At points I've been in multiple groups at a time. As time goes on, people move away or their schedules change. If it's supported by a theater, they may bring the group to an end to make room for a new set of people. So sometimes you have to scramble to find a new group. Four to eight is a good number if people show up regularly—maybe more than eight if they don't show up regularly. I got to know a lot of writers this way. Playwrights often help each other out and tell each other about theaters or opportunities you might not know about. Many times, a playwright has shared a play of mine with someone in the industry. Playwrights helping playwrights are the best kind of playwrights. And it can be fun to talk shop.

Right now I'm in a parents writing group with Project Y Theatre. It's nice to talk about playwriting alongside parenting challenges. When people can't come because of a sick kid or babysitting issue, we all get it. We meet once a month and one person brings a full play.

I'm also in a Zoom group with Flux Theater Ensemble where people bring in ten pages or so every two weeks. My wife is also in the group and now so is my ten-year-old son, and there's a girl around his age who is the daughter of two members of the theater and both of the kids are writing plays and casting themselves in each other's plays, too. Usually we read five minutes of kid plays and then get into the adult stuff.

I may start a group of my own here in Connecticut if I can find enough playwrights to be in it and who are willing to travel to wherever we meet.

Both of the groups I'm in start with a check-in where everyone says how they are and what's going on with them, and it ends with a check-out in which people lift up moments from the play or plays that will stay with them or that affected them.

I don't lead either of these groups, but when I do lead groups I do exactly what my friend Michelle Bossy did when she led the Primary Stages writing group: I ask the writer sharing if they want to say anything before we read. I have them cast the show from the people in the room. We read the play and then, afterward, we clap. If it's one long play we might take a bathroom break. If not, I will say to the playwright, "Great! What would you like to know?" or "Do you have questions for us?" or "What do you want to talk about?" That way, the playwright leads the discussion. If they want only compliments, we give only compliments. If they want to know where we were confused, we say that.

If there are plays containing slurs or anything like that, the playwright should mention that before the play is read so as not to surprise people. Usually, it's best not to say those words out loud out of consideration for everyone in the room. Also if there are any content considerations, such as a play containing suicidal ideation, the playwright should mention that, too.

A writing group is a sacred space and it's important to only invite people who you trust and are dedicated to keeping comments and questions constructive.

Sometimes when I have a writing group in class, I check in to make sure the student whose play is read isn't overwhelmed by the notes. Sometimes you can see on their face: they have enough thoughts and are overwhelmed. Be careful not to monologue or overwhelm your peers.

DRAMATURGS AND DRAMATURGICAL DIRECTORS

Do you already know what a dramaturg is? Sometimes the literary manager at the theater is also the production dramaturg. There are also freelance dramaturgs.

Dramaturgs sometimes do research for casts during productions or for playwrights on various aspects of their play. Sometimes there's a lot of background the cast and the director need about the time period or specific world of the play. My plays don't usually have a lot of that, so often the dramaturg, if there is one, doesn't have a lot to do in that regard.

Dramaturgs can also be really good at helping you with the storytelling aspects of your play. They can be another set of eyes looking for parts that are confusing or moments that aren't landing.

It can be very helpful to have a good dramaturg in the room when you are workshopping a new play. Sometimes you may want to hire one to help you with your play. I have worked with lots of different dramaturgs but also most of the time I don't work with anyone at all.

If you find a dramaturg you love, hold onto them and figure out how to work with them as much as you can. Likewise, some directors are very good at storytelling and are helpful to have directing a new play that needs some work. There is an actor I like to work with a lot on new work because she asks questions about all the moments and really kicks all the tires of my play.

People don't use the phrase "dramaturgical actor," but she's really a dramaturgical actor. Lots of actors are helpful if they are able to tell you when they're getting stuck or finding it difficult to connect one thought with the next when working on a part.

Some playwrights are very good dramaturgs for other play-wrights within a writing group setting, or when doing a play swap where you read each other's plays and then talk about them.

REVISING YOUR PLAY

How do you go about revising so your play becomes more of what it should be? You're making things clearer where they need to be clear. You're looking at character arcs: are they functioning how they're supposed to? Is the audience getting the right information at the right time, or should something come earlier or later? You're cutting lines and scenes you don't need. Maybe you're even cutting characters. Most playwrights don't cut enough. Bear in mind the phrase "Kill your darlings." The "darlings" you need to delete are not the best parts of the play that you and everyone else loves. They are things you can't let go of that are getting in the way of the play functioning.

Is your play saying what you want it to say, or are people understanding something different from what you mean? Are the jokes funny enough? For me, most revisions are about clarifying and streamlining things. Is the ending satisfying (if it's supposed to be satisfying)?

How can you chip away at your block of marble to make the play the most of what it wants to be? Fix it, but don't lose the stuff that makes it good to begin with. Is there something wrong with the character, or did the actor just do it wrong? If you have to see another reading before you're sure how to revise, set up another reading. Some of my plays have lots and lots and lots of revisions, others just a few. Every play is different. Writing the next one will be different than writing the last one and revising it will be different too.

Remember: it's your play. No one can tell you what your play should be. But people can tell you their experience of your play. Sometimes prescriptive notes are wrong, and sometimes they are right but they feel wrong because they're prescriptive. Always avoid giving prescriptive notes to other writers for this reason.

Sometimes you get stuck rewriting and rewriting and rewriting the same play when you need some time away from it to see what it is. Don't look at it for a month or three. Write something else and then, when you come back to it, you can sometimes better see what it is and isn't.

WORKSHOPPING A PLAY

The word "workshop" means so many different things in the play world that I'm not sure I could tell you what someone means when they say they had a workshop of their play. Did they do a rehearsed reading? Was it a staged reading—that is, with the actors holding scripts in their hands and the director having added some movement beyond just standing up for entrances and sitting down for exits? I had a very helpful two-week rehearsal that ended in a reading at a LORT a few years back. The play got so much better through that process. I wish I could get more things like that, but they're rare. (For me, anyway.)

People sometimes also use the word "workshop" to describe a bare-bones production where the actors learned their lines and performed in front of an audience for a couple of performances. I love workshop productions, which I like to call "productions that don't count." There aren't reviews, so you can see what the play is but you can fix what isn't working before the next iteration. I recently had a college production that I'm thinking of here, though the design aspects of it were really great. It was fully staged with a large, friendly audience, but I don't have to call that a premiere unless I want to.

Some theaters still want to say they're staging the world premiere of a play even though their audiences don't care as much about that. I think it's a status thing—or, depending on the size of the theater, they may be able to get a percentage of your royalties on the play for the next five years or so. I try to avoid giving that away if I can: the royalties are already so small that after the agent gets ten percent (or twenty percent for an amateur production), I don't want to give away another five percent or two percent or whatever they're asking for.

Apropos of none of this, but sort of related: Back in the day, I once had a reading in which only one audience member showed up. That was not helpful for getting the vibe of the audience during different parts of the show to see what was and wasn't working. Please go to your friend's readings so this doesn't happen to them.

THE SUBCONSCIOUS

Remember when I said it's not magic? Also, sometimes writing is magic. Your subconscious knows stuff you don't know. It knows how to solve the problems in your play. Sometimes you just have to let it work while you're sleeping or washing the dishes. Don't push it. It will come. Do think about the problem before you go to sleep. Do forget about the problem and take a shower.

Let your subconscious talk to you about unrelated stuff. Write that stuff down and wonder at it. Try freewriting, where you just put your pen to the paper and don't stop writing for five or ten or thirty minutes. It doesn't matter what you write. Just keep going. Sometimes interesting things come this way.

MEET PEOPLE

Writing a play is solitary, but making theater isn't. Playwrights are often introverts. But you need relationships to get your plays up there in the world. You have to put yourself in situations where you are forced to talk to strangers. You should be trying to meet directors and actors and literary people at theaters. Other playwrights are often generous about introducing their friends to actors and directors. So make all kinds of theater friends, for yourself and for the community.

If in-person is hard or you live far away from some of the people you want to meet, there are also online communities. Be a good community member online and in person. Show up to readings and tell people when you like what they're doing. Ask people to go to plays with you. Form or join a writing group. If you see plays regularly, you will sometimes see some of the same people over and over. The theater world is small. Introduce yourself. Offer your friendship. Don't ask for anything when first meeting someone.

There is some truth to "It's all who you know." It helps to know everyone. Sometimes plays get done because someone likes your play and sometimes they like your play but you're also their friend. Some of the people who are your peers now will go on to become the heads of theaters. They will become Artistic Directors and TV showrunners. Some of them will be very famous someday, or at least in a position to do your play, if you have the right play at the right time that is right for their theater. You shouldn't expect this from them. Most of them are friends with way more people than they can program at their theater. But know the friendships and acquaintances you make now may help you in the future. So many first productions staged Off-Off-Broadway or regionally came about because of a director or an actor who I gave my play to and who made it happen. Yes, people may help you someday, and hopefully you can also help people. Look for how you can help people whose work you like and who you like. The theater runs on us connecting each other and helping each other. We rise together. And keep being nice. Someone you will not remember meeting may remember you ten years from now.

WHETHER TO GO TO GRAD SCHOOL

A question I get a lot is, "Should I go to grad school?" Grad school gave me a reason to move to New York City, where I found collaborators, an artistic life, and other theater people. It allowed me to eat, breathe, and talk theater and playwriting for three years of my life. It also put me in A LOT of debt.

If you do choose to apply to grad schools, I have two main recommendations: don't go into a lot of debt, and manage your expectations of what it can do for your career. You are lucky in that there are a lot more free or cheap grad schools for playwriting than there were when I went to school. But the expensive ones are a lot more expensive than they used to be. There are also just a lot more MFA playwriting programs overall, including low-residency programs.

Like with everything, research the schools well. Talk to alums if you can. Read plays by the professors. Find out what you can about how they teach. Most grad schools will not help your career in any real way. Maybe you will meet collaborators and maybe you will become a better writer, but for the most part you won't leave with an agent or an impressive production. There are a couple schools that get a little more attention than others—Yale, Juilliard, maybe UCSD. Sometimes your professor can help you a little in your career. Sometimes they don't really have that power. And so much is about timing and luck.

So what I am trying to say is that grad school is not going to make or break your career. If you don't take that path, figure out on your own how to write better and meet people. And be somewhere where the theater is, for at least a little while.

AFTER GRAD SCHOOL

Sometimes, after grad school, you have to rediscover your voice again. This happens to actors who go through training: they hear all the voices in their head of their teachers telling them to remember this or that they're doing that wrong and they have to find who they are and what they do best again. For me, it was finding my comedic voice again, but for you it could be something else. I had to stop trying to be funny to get to a new place in my writing, and then I had to get my funny back again. Maybe that won't happen to you. I hope it won't. But, look, we're all evolving all the time.

WHERE SHOULD I LIVE?

Where as a playwright should you live? First of all, where do you as a human want to live? Is there theater nearby? If not, maybe find a place you can stand where there is theater. Some small cities have active theater scenes and some don't. Chicago has a huge theater ecosystem. I haven't spent a lot of time there but I hear it is an amazing place to make theater. But the media isn't there, so people outside Chicago may not know what you're doing. LA's theater scene is very spread out but is also very active; it also is dwarfed by the giant TV and film industries. Whenever I have even a small play in LA, there are always understudies for every single part, because at any time someone could get a job and have to leave to film something. Minneapolis, Philly, Cleveland, Cincinnati, New Orleans, and DC are all fun places to make theater. And I'm sure there are many, many more. Ideally, find a place that has one or two large theaters and more than a few smaller theaters and get involved. Volunteer, help, or work for them. Make your own work. Become a good-size fish in a small pond.

Or go to a big pond like New York, where there is Broadway, Off-Broadway and Off-Off-Broadway, and the media covers a lot of it. I don't know if it's still possible to get the *New York Times* to come to a three-week run in a tiny space, but it was when I was starting out. With a little luck. And if you hired a PR person.

But also, what kind of plays are you trying to make, and where does the audience for those plays live? And where will you be happy living? How can you have a life in the theater and also have a life that you want?

Life is long. When you're young, it's easier to make art late into the night and live with five roommates. Can you spend some time doing that and learn what you can in a place with a lot of theater? Or is that not what your life should be? Listen to your gut, but don't give into fear of the unknown.

TEN YEARS

My former professor, Tish Dace, told me it took ten years to get anywhere as a playwright. I think this is a good way to look at it. If you're working hard in all the right ways for ten years, you will probably see some progress. I feel like at about year eight there was a shift for me. And things did get a little easier.

I still wish a lot of things were easier right now. I'm not sure there's a moment where I will ever say, "Oh now I can relax. The hustle is over." In fact, I feel like I ran into ageism at a certain point, where some things had definitely become easier but other things became harder and I was no longer included among the shiny new writers.

All kinds of things can help prevent you from getting what you want. Racism is huge. Sexism is huge. Timing is important and completely out of our hands. When you're young, you're too young. When you're older, you're too old. So, depending on your luck and who you are, your ten years could be five years or fifteen years. Everyone's path is different. Keep your head down and keep at it. And, like in a play, there is cause and effect. The effect comes from the work you put in and put out into the world. But it takes time. Often, when people describe writing careers, they say it's a marathon, not a sprint. Keep going. And know please that the effort you put in will almost never have the effect you want *when* you want it. Only the very few and the very lucky get any kind of fame or a large amount of money from this. But maybe it's enough to see your play in front of an audience. Maybe it's enough to get an email from someone who read your play and loved it.

AVOID DATING YOUR PLAY

By which I mean avoid putting references in your play that may seem dated in a few years. I don't mean don't go on a date with your play. Totally, take your play out for a night on the town if it makes you happy, but when writing, try not to use too many celebrity names or products or jokes about what's happening now. It might take you more than five years to get the play produced, and some of the jokes might not still be funny. Pop culture references that are too specific could date the play and make people not want to produce it anymore. The goal is always to have a play that continues to feel contemporary and talks about what we all care about now, for as long as it's possible.

All that said, you can't completely prevent your play from feeling dated down the road. The ways we talk about ideas change. Technology changes. Slang changes. But, as much as possible, I try to not include references in my plays that will feel dated in a couple of years. And it mostly works. I have plays I wrote ten, fifteen, even twenty years ago that are still done.

By the way, I know I have dated myself in this book. I've already written about Facebook a few times. Odds are many of you don't use Facebook. It could disappear in the next five years. I should probably be talking about TikTok and how you can use that or whatever the new thing that doesn't exist yet that everyone will be using three years from now. Harness the future, playwrights.

But you can only write your work in the present. Part of your job as a writer is to write all your plays before you die and to let the future know what it's like to be alive now. Personally, I think the future doesn't need to know how you feel about what's going on with Taylor Swift* right now, but if that or something else right this second is important to your work, ignore what I'm saying and do it your way. Just know that old slang or gossip or news may limit future productions of your work.

*(To my student who wrote a play about Taylor Swift: I'm not talking about you. I really like that play a lot.)

IMPOSTER SYNDROME; OR, THE QUESTION OF CONFIDENCE

You need confidence to start writing and finish a play. You need confidence to email people to ask them to read your play. You also need a good amount of self-criticism to work on your play and to become a better writer. For some people the problem is too much confidence, which makes them blind to the flaws in their writing. For other people, the problem is not enough confidence, and they have trouble finishing their plays or putting their work out there. For all of this to work, a balance is necessary. Or, if you can't find balance, find the ability to seesaw between the ridiculous amount of self-confidence you need and the humility to accept when your play comes short of what you want it to be.

Imposter syndrome, in my experience, never totally goes away. But it has gotten better for me. I'm no longer terrified that in rehearsal actors will show me a fatal flaw that makes it obvious to everyone that my play is terrible. (Mostly.) The fact that I'm even writing this book means I've come a long way with my own imposter syndrome. (Although I keep thinking, "Who am I to write a book? Is this going to actually be helpful for anyone?" But I'm just going to push through that.)

It helps to have years of people taking you seriously as a playwright. I can stand in front of a class and answer questions about playwriting, but I never stop seeing what my plays aren't. I never stop wondering about their worth. I do read most reviews—one time, so I have an idea of what people do and don't like about a specific play. And sometimes I can feel pretty strongly that they're wrong and also feel pretty bad about what they wrote.

No play is for everybody. And people will sometimes think your choices point to flaws in your art. And you aren't there to tell them, "No, I did that on purpose. I like it that way." Not that it would matter if you could say that to them. There is a huge range of kinds of stories and people may love you as a person but not like your stories all that much. That is okay. It's normal. Try not to take it personally if you can. It's not about you, or even about your play, usually. We all like different things. My wife really likes some of my plays. A few of them, I think, are part of why she fell in love with me and I know her writing is part of why I fell in love with her. But after twenty years together, we don't always love everything the other writes. She is not my biggest fan, I'm sure. In fact, she has never read a lot of plays of mine, and some of the others I know she's not crazy about. That's fine. It helps keep me grounded.

And I hope that for you, too: enough people saying nice things about your work to chip away at your imposter syndrome and sharing enough helpful notes about your plays for you to be able to see all the facets of what they are and aren't and be able to improve what needs improving.

I should say that, as a white cis male, my battle with imposter syndrome is probably not as fierce a battle as many of you have to face. It's okay to ask for help from someone smart and confident if you need to compose an email or work on your synopsis. Stand next to your confident friend, who will sing your praises in public. Or do the thing that takes confidence even when you're not feeling that way. Faking confidence is sometimes necessary.

WRITING ABOUT PERSONAL THINGS

Every writer should be able to write exactly what they want to. That doesn't mean that once you show it to people they have to like it or that it won't cause problems. When you write autobiographically, you may run into people in your life who are upset by your play. I know a writer who had a very real concern about how the government of his home country would react to a production of his play. Consequences are real. Some plays can sever relationships. That isn't a reason not to write them. But it may be a reason to not invite someone to your reading. It may be a reason not to tell your family the details of your play. Eugene O'Neill famously wrote *Long Day's Journey into Night* and gave it to his wife as a wedding present, forbidding her from ever producing it and saying it could only be published twenty-five years after his death. She ignored his wishes and we are the richer for that play.

I'm in a phase in my writing where I don't write much that's literally autobiographical, and I think my plays are better for it. There are ways to disguise characters based on real people. Changing their gender sometimes works. Using some specifics that are clearly not them can help. Sometimes people see themselves in plays when the plays are not about them. There's not a lot you can do about that. Make friends who are in the theater or art world who may be more understanding about these things. But also leave behind toxic relationships. Don't let terrible people keep you from making the art you want to make. Or figure out how to have the conversation with people who you want in your life. My advice is to be brave but also consider what you are willing to lose and not lose.

TV AND FILM OR MUSICALS OR NOVELS OR POETRY AND MORE

If you get burnt out writing plays or just want to try something else, try to learn how to write a pilot or feature film or a musical or novel or poem. Many playwrights I know also write in other media. For each one, there's a steep learning curve. They are all vastly different kinds of writing. Sometimes some of the skills from playwriting carry over, but there are new skills specific to each kind that you need to learn in order to excel.

There are lots of books that can help you learn how to do these things better and lots of articles and podcasts you can Google. Below is a very brief primer on what I know about each medium. I've done a little of all of these and I feel like I can say a little about all of them except poetry. I have no good advice for you on your poems.

TV and film are visual media. The scenes are a lot shorter. A three-page scene would be a very long scene. You have to get more done in a shorter period of time. And, for the most part, a lot more has to happen. Also, structure is very important. If structure isn't your strength, this will be hard for you. A lot of playwrights make very good TV and film writers, but some can't make that leap. Get in and out of scenes quickly and make sure the plot is always moving. Always have a B story. Read lots of scripts, which are easy to find online. Break down the act structures of your favorites. Notice how much more is left unsaid on the screen than in the theater. If you don't live in LA or have an agent or a manager for TV or film, it will be really hard to break in.

You can self-produce short films or web series with people who know what they're doing, or you can all learn together. Your short film can be a calling card of sorts to show people you want to work with, but very rarely can anyone be hired on a TV show from a short film. It can still help you learn how to do the thing.

Playwrights have an advantage in the TV world because we already know how to talk to actors, and a TV set is similar in a lot of ways to working in a theater with a director. We already write good dialogue and characters. If you can figure out how to translate what you do well onstage to the screen, you may have a good career in the TV or film world.

I wrote a couple of novels and learned a lot by doing that. I am no way an expert at that kind of writing. Michael Chabon and Stephen King both wrote great books on writing fiction containing lots of advice, some of which is applicable to playwriting, too. With both screenwriting and fiction writing, it's harder for me to find my flow. The writing is slower and harder. But like with everything, as you keep doing it, it does get easier and you can find a rhythm. I outline a novel as if I'm writing a feature film, with a three-act structure. Lots of authors want their novels to be made into films, so I thought that if I had enough beats for a film, I would have almost enough for a novel. I wrote in first person and past tense, because as a playwright, first person makes the most sense to me and I assumed I would be better at it. I wanted to write in present tense, but past tense is more standard and present tense is still jarring to a lot of readers. (Really, I wanted to write in second person, but that would be even more jarring, don't you think?) That first novel was the hardest thing I ever tried to write.

If you want to feel like you've accomplished something, write a novel.

Like TV, fiction is a whole other world with a lot to learn about writing and publishing. You can spend hours reading articles and books about writing and publishing books. There is a very active online community of writers that you can get involved in if you want to take this path.

I am also a beginner at writing musicals. The person who structures a musical and writes all the dialogue is called the book writer or librettist. Most playwrights handle that part, but some also write lyrics. Again, structure is important. If this is a thing you want to do, watch a lot of musicals and read the book *The Secret Life of the American Musical*. Even more so than with plays, there can be a mystery to why some musicals work and others don't. An effective musical a very finely tuned machine. Generally it takes at least five years to work and rework one, but it can easily take ten or more. Like in a screenplay, musical dialogue is concise and focused, and the book takes a backseat to the flashier, more fun songs. If you turn a play of yours into a musical like I just did, you will find that most of the great lines and exciting scenes become songs. So writing the book is much more of a thankless job, but when it works, it pays really well. And musicals can be so much fun.

Other kinds of writing playwrights tackle include advertising copy, graphic novels, audio dramas, video games, live televised events, and nonfiction books about playwriting. People write for reality shows, soap operas, wrestling. Writers are necessary everywhere. If you get excited about something else, go try it out. The theater will still be here when you get back, if you want to come back.

ON CAREGIVING

I was the primary caregiver for almost the first two years of my child's life, while my wife was working full-time running a youth theater. I know that taking care of a child or a parent or spouse or relative can make having a playwriting career really hard. This is especially true for women, who are expected still to do much more than men in both household tasks and childcare. I think caregiving is so very important, but your artistic life is, too.

None of us can have it all, but try hard to get what you need within the world of what is possible. Ask for help. That's really hard for some of us to do, but no one can do everything themselves. If you have a partner, do what you can to get them to do their equal share of the household and childcare tasks. Ask for what you need as an artist and know there will always be too many chores and never enough time for you to do your work. There will always be times you want to get away to work on something and you just can't because of a job or caregiving or both.

I was lucky at one point to live near my mother, who could watch my son for a couple hours while I went to the coffee shop to write or when I would go to the city for my writing group. Not everyone has that. But everyone needs that. Figure out what you can get. Figure out breaks for yourself and schedule "artist dates." Keep your artistic soul alive.

Also, know that you don't have to have a kid. Having a kid makes your artistic life a lot harder for at least fifteen to twenty years. Think about what you want your life to look like, if you have a choice in the matter.

ON BEING MARRIED
TO A PLAYWRIGHT

I am married to a playwright. And my wife is an amazing person to be married to. Should you date a playwright? Depends. Do you fall in love with artists? Can you handle being romantically entangled with someone who maybe will become more successful at the thing you want to do? I like to tell people it's hard being a playwright on the day you both get the same rejection email and it says different things. One of you will always be doing better than the other. Can you cope with that jealousy in your own home? If so, you'll also have someone who will understand your frustrations without needing them explained. Someone who you can share theater jokes with, who will want to go see a play with you and will love theater as much as you love theater—and maybe give you detailed notes about your play or help you write your synopsis or tell the world when you have a play coming out. I know a lot of playwrights who are married to each other. And I know a lot of playwrights who are much happier dating someone supportive who is not part of that world.

Also, dating a lot in the theater world is common but be aware you will probably run into them at theater events, especially if you have a lot of theater exes. And if you're a love-'em-and-leave-'em sort, you could get a bad reputation in the theater world.

And you don't have to get married or anything, but if you do, maybe marry well. It's not a terrible idea to link up with someone who has health insurance and a stable income.

QUESTIONS STUDENTS ASK WHEN I'M VISITING A CLASS

You should probably be prepared to answer these questions, too.

Who are your favorite playwrights?
Honestly, there are too many to name. Early on, when I was just starting to write, I read everything I could find by Christopher Durang and Nicky Silver. They formed my idea of what comedy could be in theater.

This is how I'm doing this character. Am I doing it right?
Yes.

What's your favorite character in this play? (Asked in a room full of actors who are all playing characters in the play.)
(I rarely actually have a favorite character in a play. I mean, when I'm writing it, I'm playing all of them in my head. But I usually say someone anyway. If it's a play with a big cast, I like to say it's one of the characters that's not on stage the whole time.)

What's your favorite book?
I have no idea. Right now I'm reading a book called *My Year of Living Danishly*, but most of the time I read fiction that has nothing to do with what I'm writing. I don't reread books much, but

Nobody's Fool is one book that I have read a few times. I read young adult, graphic novels, rom-coms, fantasy, literary fiction. I had never read Jane Austen until recently, when I read all of her books.

What's your favorite color?
Blue.

What do you do about writer's block?
Wake up and write first thing. Take a shower or a walk or sit in front of a fan. Take a break. Come back to it later. Or sit there and write about it in your notebook. Meditate. Run or do yoga or whatever you do.

When did you start writing plays?
I started in earnest on a summer break after my sophomore year of college. And I've always written plays since then.

How did you become a writer?
I was an actor and when I started writing, plays were the easiest for me to write.

(Sometimes the underlying question here is "Can I do what you did too?" Sometimes I feel like they're looking for the secret to art or fame or something else. In high school and college, they're at an age where everything seems possible but it's all so far away. I don't know if it's helpful, but I try to assure them I'm a human like anyone else.)

What's your inspiration for this play? / Where do you get your ideas?
(It's really helpful to have an answer for that question because you will get it a lot. Sometimes I don't remember very well. So I basically say the following ...)

I keep notebooks where I write ideas down and at all times I'm thinking about what I want to write and when I have enough helpful notes about something and know how it begins and ends and a bunch of the middle and what it's about, I start writing it.

What's the message of your play?
(By this, they also mean, "What is the thesis of your play?")

You're not writing an essay. A play is very rarely persuasive writing. You don't have to have a thesis. That doesn't mean your play shouldn't be about something.

(However, students writing essays can try to come up with their own ideas about the themes and theses of our plays. I just think teachers sometimes steer students wrong about what art is and does. And sometimes that creates a tension in the classroom I'm visiting, in which the student wants a pat answer to a question that doesn't have a pat answer.)

When I started writing, it was in fashion for plays to kind of argue both sides of an issue and it was seen as a moral failing if it was too skewed in one direction, as if the play was a form of journalism. And you still see that kind of play sometimes. Some people write plays from perspectives we haven't seen before or teach the audience about a world they may not know about. But a lot of plays are not trying to convince the audience of anything. And that's okay. Sometimes you may have a thesis for a play, but maybe it's not one you want to tell anyone about, like "Love will tear you apart" or "Kindness can heal." Maybe the overwhelming takeaway is a worldview about the nature of humanity. Or the darkness and whether or not it will win.

Aristotle, of course, had very clear ideas about what a play should be in *Poetics*. His version of tragedy can be very powerful. Arthur Miller certainly built phenomenal tragedies with Aristotle's building blocks. But that kind of play, in which a character's fatal flaw leads to a fated downfall, never felt true to me. If it feels true to you, don't let me sway you. Again, figure out what you want your play to be and make that kind of play. Do you admire plays of ideas or symbolism or lots of twists and turns? Find what you like most and figure out how to make your version of that.

BE IN THE ROOM

As much as you can, try to be part of the conversations that a theater is having when producing your play. If you have time to attend, tell them you want to go to marketing meetings and design meetings and production meetings. Partially, this will help you to know what those meetings are like and understand the amount of work that goes into everything. You can also see drawings of the set and ensure it makes sense before they build it. Find out where costuming is headed, too. Usually the playwright is not part of these conversations, but let them know you are interested while not being a pain in the ass, and you may help see problems that you can help solve. Be part of the solution, not the problem.

I'm doing a show right now where I live far away from the theater and couldn't be around for the last week and a half, and during that time a lot of decisions were made without my input. For the most part, they did an awesome job without me, but there is a costume choice I don't love that probably can't be changed at this point.

There will always be things that aren't exactly the way you want them to be. Collaboration involves inevitable give and take. You should absolutely argue for and, if necessary, fight for your vision. But also live within the reality of what is possible. And continue to be collaborative and generous and kind. Sometimes a small production will already have an actor or director attached and if you say no, the production is no longer happening. So you have to balance, for example, an actor who isn't quite right against the possibility that the play you wrote won't get staged. Sometimes you may regret compromising artistically, like when you think you really need a production but the production you get is too far from what the play wants to be. I am lucky in that this has almost never happened to me with productions in which I am directly involved.

It's important to be as involved as you can be with the first, and maybe second, production of the play. After that, I let it go out into the world and hope for the best. I find people either understand how the play should be or don't. And there's not a lot you can do about it.

WRITE ABOUT LOVE

Write a scene about two people falling in love. Send it to me. I
love that shit.

YOU CAN PULL YOUR PLAY

Once I had a play in London and the production made a lot of choices that didn't make sense. One actor was doing a Brooklyn accent, but his character was supposed to be from Vermont. An actress was wearing a dress that appeared to be a wedding dress. But mostly the production was too slow. The tone was wrong and none of the comedy was funny. The magic that I think the play hinges on was absent. The director also moved some of the dialogue to form monologues in a different part of the play. They assured me that everyone was loving it. And the audience—made up mostly of friends of the company—did seem to really enjoy the play. But my English friend, who was not a theater person, definitely hated it. I told the director what I thought about the tone and that I didn't like the dialogue being moved around. Contractually, of course, he was not allowed to do that. He told me that he had fixed my play.

They needed my permission to remount the play in what is basically the London version of Off-Broadway. I hated what they did to my play. I thought that if I let them put it up, it would get torn apart by reviewers and they would assume the play they saw was my play. So I didn't let them do that. That was twelve years ago, and neither that play nor any other play of mine has since received a big London production. I said no to a good amount of money and a big production for artistic reasons. And maybe that bad production could have led to something good, but I seriously doubt it.

YOU CAN PULL YOUR PLAY

Did I make the right move? I think so. If people hate my play, I want them to hate a version of what the play is supposed to be. If they love it, I want them to love the play I intend too.

And if anyone changes your play without your permission, you have the right to stop the production from continuing. Standard contracts all say only the playwright can change the script.

USE A DRAMATISTS GUILD CONTRACT

If you're a US playwright, join the Dramatists Guild for solidarity and for the magazine *The Dramatist* and for submission listings, but also for the free contract boilerplates and the lawyers who will check your contract for you and tell you if there are issues.

As playwrights, we have rights, and you should know about them. No one can change your words without your permission. You have the right to be at any rehearsal. Check out the "Bill of Rights" on the Guild website (www.dramatistsguild.com).

As soon as you write the play, it is copyrighted. You own it. When you let someone stage it, you are renting it out to them and they pay you royalties in return.

Some writers pay money to register their script at the copyright office or at the Writers Guild of America page. I don't do this. Plays don't make much money, so stealing them is a waste of a thief's time. Publishers will register the copyright of your play for you as part of the publication process. Basically, I don't think anyone will bother to steal my play, and if they do, they probably won't know how to use it to make money. But if it makes you feel better, go ahead and register your work at the copyright office.

ALL THE THINGS

Bixby Elliot, a playwriting peer of mine, introduced to me his three-pronged approach: at any given time he is writing a new play, submitting a play, and trying to produce a play. This isn't for everyone, and I don't think it's sustainable for anyone unless you have a lot of support. But I think it shows the nature of a playwriting career, where you're always writing new things while working on getting already written things out into the world. Revision happens while writing, while submitting. So it's common to hop from a new thing you're writing to revising a play you wrote five years ago and then emailing your bio that someone asked for two weeks ago for a reading of a play you wrote two years ago and whose director wants to talk on the phone about that play, and it's hard to remember who you were when you wrote that play and you're not sure what to say.

Which brings me to administrative tasks. There are lots of administrative tasks that come with the career. I always underestimate how much time these things take. You could spend days in auditions for a play and hours talking about casting. You might even have to create sides for auditions sometimes. There are lots of conversations about casting for readings, and you have to go into your emails and records to find the perfect actor for something. Writing statements for development opportunities, revising your bio and resume, and setting up coffee dates all take effort and time. You have to fill out W9s and nudge people to pay you for things they said they would pay you for. Sometimes a school visit is as easy as a check in the mail, and sometimes it requires you to fill out an elaborate online form. There are so many emails that happen for everything you do and that's all very time-consuming. I've had interns a couple of times, and I know some of my peers who are extremely busy in TV or on Broadway hire assistants just because there are always so many tiny tasks to take care of for every event, production, reading, or school visit.

I hope that you someday get to hire an assistant. Until then, you need to figure out a way to get writing done as well as all the admin as well as revising and submitting and doing your day job while also having time to do normal life things. I think it's helpful to batch all the tiny tasks together. Send all the scripts at the same time. Put time aside in your day to respond to emails. Whatever works for you. But know that it's part of the life and part of the job and it always takes more time than you think it will.

GENRE PLAY MY WAY

I'm going to tell you how I write a genre play. This may or may not be helpful to you. Either way, this is what I do.

So, the thing I'm often doing is writing about the genre as well as in the genre. I'll be writing a comedy—maybe it's a parody, but that word has negative connotations—that's an explosion of a genre that should be funny and also should be its own thing. You don't need to make it a comedy, however, unless that's what you do.

It could be a film noir or pirate story or western or Elizabethan drama or comic book play. Something that takes place in space. Whatever genre you love. I don't write horror, but horror onstage is a lot of fun. Suspense. Ancient Greek. True crime. Take a genre that is known and do your own thing to it. People like the familiar and they like being surprised, so this is a way to give them both of those things. And also use it to say what you want to say.

First, study the genre. Watch a bunch of movies or read a bunch of books. The point of this is to find the genre touchstones and the archetypes so that you can take them and make them your own, creating something that is familiar while being unique.

So, if I want to write a pirate play, for example, the expected things are swordfights, cannons, life on a ship, a parrot, a treasure map, an eye patch, a peg leg, masculinity. Maybe a storm. A kidnapping. A ship run aground on a desert island. Now I take those fun elements and I figure out which ones belong in the story I want to tell and what unique things that are not usually in this kind of story should go in mine so that it will feel new. Now, if you want to write about masculinity, a pirate play is a good place to do that. In fact, it was done really well on TV recently in the show *Our Flag Means Death*.

The thing to do is figure out what you like to write about and find a new genre arena that matches the concerns and interests in your work. Do you want to write about human connection using robots? Do you want to use Victorian romance to write about class?

Some of my most successful and least successful plays are genre plays. Do with that what you will.

SOMETHING THAT CAN
SCREW YOU UP

Many times I have had productions that seemed like they were going to happen fall through for one reason or another. The more exciting the planned production, the more it has the potential to mess with your head when it falls through. Most of the time, you never find out why it didn't happen. A lot of the time it's because of money.

Sometimes I have a reading of a play that goes really well. The audience seems to love it. The artists love it. The actors compliment your writing and your play and the talkback goes great. It's a lovefest. And then there's silence from the producing organization. Sometimes this happens over and over, and for no clear reason that you can figure out, a play that seems like a big hit in a reading can't get a production.

And, look, it's really easy to take it in and get really discouraged. Your ego comes into play and the injustice and the sometimes arbitrary nature of what gets done and what doesn't can make you think that you're a tortured genius who will never be recognized in your own time. And look, you *could* be a tortured genius. It's possible there are a lot of tortured geniuses in the theater. Maybe.

The reality is, there are a lot of good plays. I have a lot of plays that I think are really good that are sitting on my shelf, never performed.

All you can do is keep plugging away. Keep writing. Keep sending your plays to people. Produce your own work if you can. Theaters and theater companies want what they want. Most of the time it has nothing to do with you or with furthering your career. They just have different priorities and serve their audience. Maybe they need a play for a certain actor or director or they want a play about something other than what you've written.

In other words, you can only do what you can do. Do your best to write your best play and get your work out into the world. It's possible your best play may never see the light of day if you don't produce it yourself. The theatrical universe is not merit-based. Sometimes it's just about marketing. At other points it's timing or just not having found the champion for your play yet. But the biggest champion for your play is always going to be you. Take it seriously.

Tomorrow there will be another reading of an exciting play by someone else. And if you're free, go see it if you can and laugh and cry along with everyone else. Because theater is a community.

JEALOUSY

We all rise together, but also we totally don't. As much as you can, cheer on the successes of your peers. It's helpful to know, though, that their success may seem bigger than your own success just because it's not yours. It's a thing you didn't get. We are all going to get different things at different times, and by the time you get the thing you get, it will no longer seem like it's as big a deal as it did before you got the thing. We get used to the new normal. Please try to remind yourself of this weird way our minds work against us. Because the super-cool things we want are so much more amazing than what they become once we actually get them.

And a great production can have so many things go wrong along the way. The wrong casting, wrong director, bad marketing. It's magic when all the things go well. So when someone else gets that thing, know that they are living in the reality of what that actually is and when you get something cool happening, you will live in the reality. And the reality entails all the steps you did to make that thing happen. It might be a thing you built from the ground up or it might be a small windfall after years of toiling. And it might not be so great once you're actually living it. It might actually be a terrible theater to work at. I don't hope that for you. I wish you wonderful people to work with, but from the outside, someone's awesome thing looks awesome and sometimes the reality is that it's not that great.

It's like how many of us present ourselves on social media, where we only show our successes. We all know that's not the day-to-day reality, but it feels like it is. I remember my first *New York Times* review. It was a good review and I thought it would probably change something. I was at my office job when I read the review and I was thrilled and then I had to go make photocopies for someone. My day-to-day life was the same. And, yes, some people bought tickets to the show who otherwise wouldn't have. They laughed in recognition at the line in the play that was quoted in the review. And basically there was no big effect on my career.

I had other good reviews after that and maybe some of them led to out-of-town productions in small theaters, or to someone knowing about me or the play who otherwise wouldn't have. Twice I had *New York Times* Critic's Picks. They were mere months apart. And I have to say, neither of them shifted my career in the way you might expect something like that to shift your career. I've had multiple fancy readings that went really well and never led to productions. So it's easy to live in the world of what could have happened "if only…." In plays we expect cause and effect, but sometimes in our lives that just doesn't happen. You have a hit play but afterward you're almost back to where you were before. No TV show calls you up. No one offers you a commission. You win no awards. Except if you do. Some people do. Someone has to win the award. But then, after you win the award, you go back to your life again.

You will only get what you get. Most people will not get much at all so if you get anything that's a huge win.

For me, I don't win awards. It's been a while since I've had a fancy reading. But my plays are done all over. Everyone has a different idea of what success means, but a lot of times it's linked to whatever you're not getting. So be aware of that and try to not succumb to the jealousy. Paula Vogel once said to me—and I'm paraphrasing—that good work helps us all. Go, make your cool thing. The theater world needs all the good things of all fashions and stripes. It needs new and different and it needs comfortable and familiar. It needs all the kinds of plays.

Everyone's path is different and you can only leverage what you have. Do everything you have to do—write, revise, submit, invite, network—but at the end of the day, it's mostly out of your hands what happens to your work. You can only keep showing up and doing the work.

During orientation at Juilliard, I started telling the new writers that some of them would be getting new attention and opportunities and that it's hard for the people who get that new attention and it's hard for those that don't, and their job is to support each other and not become assholes.

So I say the same to you. Don't be the asshole. Support your peers. Don't let bitterness and cynicism win. It's easy to go to the theater and hate everything and rail at the bad work and get bitter that they are doing that instead of your plays. The harder thing is to not bow to jealousy. But it's a much better life.

You have to figure out what that means for you. Does it mean limiting the time you're on social media, or does it mean taking a break from seeing plays? Does it mean producing a reading series for your friends? Does it mean starting a support group for playwrights in despair? Does it mean finding a way to live a full life that isn't just about the theater? I've started running 5Ks where I live. It's a thing I'm not good at but can try to get better at. I do it with a group of people who aren't theater people and don't know me in that context. I have some non-theater friends. What is your version of that? Early on I was starved for theater people and theater conversations. Now I look for places that I don't have to talk about it. I know there's never enough time, but what can you do that isn't just more theater? I guess I'm talking about hobbies or fandom. Fishing? A book club. Whatever you like. I think it's important to not lose track of a full life while you're trying to make a career.

And that will help with the jealousy. Because your value is not linked to your playwriting success. The more people know you as a person, as a friend, the more you can be grounded and the less fame or lack of fame will affect you. Maybe I can say that because I am only treated like a famous person occasionally. But again, this is not a book for Lin Manuel Miranda.

I was in a writing group with Lin back in the day. He was a good guy and was really talented, even back then. I kind of personally know almost all the famous people in my field. So please believe me when I say I survived watching them all rise and I managed to find happiness and mostly avoid becoming bitter, and I think you can too.

UPS AND DOWNS

Every writer I know has had ups and downs, sometimes in the same day. Sometimes nothing happens for a very long time. Sometimes success is followed by silence. And that's confusing. I think the pandemic was clarifying for a lot of us artists. Most theaters shut down and acted like we didn't exist. At the end of the day, most theaters don't do a lot to support artists even in the best of times. They do the play that they think their audience wants. If you have that play then, yes, they will do that play, but next year they will do something else. And most theaters are chasing the new hot thing. Weirdly, that often means young writers who don't yet know completely how to write plays.

There are way too many of us doing good work for the number of slots in a season or in a reading series. Mostly you get a reading or a commission one time, and you may never work with that theater again. That's the norm. So if you can make a relationship with someone, you're doing great. If you have a theater or school that does more than one of your plays, that's amazing.

Many of us hope for a home. But I think the only way to do it, if you don't make that home yourself, is to try and cobble together development and productions wherever and however you can. So we apply to everything and we make our own opportunities and we try to maintain relationships and we chalk up every win we can.

It's easy to get stuck in a scarcity mindset. But good work does beget good work. It just takes longer than you think it will. And it sometimes takes a lot of work on your part long after you've reached a place where it seems like you shouldn't still have to work so hard.

DEFINE SUCCESS

I think it's helpful to define success for yourself. Once, when I was a student, I was at a party and an older established playwright asked a bunch of us what our definition of success was. I said I always wanted to have a play running somewhere. And, honestly, that's kind of been my goal, to be ubiquitous in certain circles. And it hasn't quite happened but I'm much closer to that than I used to be.

I also have defined success as getting an Off-Broadway or LORT show. Making a living from writing. Publishing a certain number of plays. Getting a good review. Writing a good play. There are so many ways to be successful, but it's also really easy to keep shifting the goalposts so that no matter what you do you will never feel successful. Because no matter what, there will be something you aren't achieving.

So please, enjoy it when you have a success. Got a complimentary rejection letter? That's a success. Someone said something nice about your play? Success. A reading where someone cried? These are all amazing things. It's a joy to hear your words for the first time coming out of the mouths of actors. Enjoy all the good things that happen as much as you can. And try not to think that your thing is not as good because it's yours. I assure you, someone wishes they had the thing that you have. Try to look at it with their eyes when you find yourself dismissing the good things that happen to you.

ALSO, FIND A
THERAPIST YOU LIKE

Really. Do this. There is a lot of pressure and a lot of ups and downs. It's helpful to talk to someone outside of the theater bubble who can provide real-world context. I don't know that any of us wouldn't do better with a therapist. Find a good one.

For years I thought I didn't need a therapist and was worried that, if I dealt with my issues, I wouldn't have anything to write about. This is nonsense. You can work on your mental health and also write well.

Mental illness and creativity can go hand in hand, but getting help with your mental health will not harm your art.

A WRITING EXERCISE

My recollection is that Eduardo Machado did a version of this on the first day of playwriting class. It is a María Irene Fornés writing exercise. Or this is his version of it. Or it's my version of his version of it. This is the thing I do most frequently when visiting a writing class. Once I make sure they all have paper and a writing utensil, I say:

> *Close your eyes. Just breathe.*

I wait a few beats here, and then I continue:

> *Imagine a door you know very well. When you can picture the door, open your eyes and draw it on your page. Don't worry about whether it's a good drawing. After you've done that, close your eyes again.*
>
> *Picture the door. Have your character look at the door. Someone or something is behind the door. When you know who or what that is, start writing.*

Then I let them write for a while. At least five or ten minutes. And I have a few versions of what comes after. You can modify it to suit your own needs. Sometimes I say:

> *There's a loud noise.*

Sometimes I say:

> *Something falls.*

But usually I say:

> *There's a knock on the door. Someone or something comes in or doesn't.*

Sometimes I say that multiple times. A writer once told me she loved that there were eventually too many people in the room because it became hard to control, so she stopped trying. And she thought it was great to have them all in there dealing with each other. I try to give them at least five or ten minutes of silent writing between my godlike utterances. Basically, you can say anything. *There's a storm,* maybe, or *a growling heard outside the door. You hear someone breathing outside the door. A window breaks. Something supernatural happens.* The vaguer and more open it is, the better, so they can twist it to their needs.

And then when the time is up I say:

> *Come to a stopping point.*

And then I ask how it went for them. For like 75 to 80 percent of the people in the room, this is an amazing exercise. Or at least they tell me it is. Eduardo said it was about opening a door to the subconscious. Or something like that. When we tried to ask him about it, he was evasive. There's something mysterious about it, I think. Maybe the mystery has to remain unsolved. And it doesn't work for everybody. But it worked for me. I don't mean that it worked for me in that I wrote amazing things while doing this exercise, but that after two or three years of exercises like this, from both Eduardo and Kelly, I had practice dredging things out of me that I didn't know were there—and it became a lot easier to dig stuff out that I cared about on a regular basis. I found that getting to emotions in writing was easier. Tapping into something inside me that I cared about was easier.

Google "maría irene fornés writing exercises" for more. There is an article in *PAJ: A Journal of Performance and Art* authored by Caridad Svich with a bunch of her exercises. She was an amazing playwright and teacher.

YOU ARE MORE THAN
A PLAYWRIGHT

I'm someone who has made my whole identity about being a playwright, interviewing playwrights, wearing shirts that say "playwright" on them, buying typewriters, endlessly talking about and seeing plays. So this is a weird thing for me to say, but there's more to life than this thing that you do. And you are more than that.

Go into the world and do the other things. Find people who don't talk about theater who you can spend time with, too. The theater world is insular and small and the actual world is gigantic and mostly unaware of us. I love to do theater, but there is so much more out there.

HOW TO NOT WRITE A PLAY

It's so fun and so easy and I forget to eat or have any fun because I'm always playwriting. How do I stop writing plays constantly?" So I wrote up this list to help you stop writing plays.

1. Take a walk. Don't take any writing implements with you. Don't think about plays. Don't write dialogue on your phone and email it to yourself.
2. Why not binge a TV show on Netflix? There are so many. You could spend hours doing that and all that time you will make sure you're not writing the play.
3. Have you had a snack? Have another one.
4. Now's a good time to clean everything. That will prevent you from writing your play.
5. Read something. Stop writing. Read an article or a book or a funny list or the Facebook status of your friend who is in an exotic place you will never be able to afford to go to.
6. Start writing something else, like an article or a poem or a short story or an essay or a book. You should really write a book anyway. Or a screenplay. Or a pilot.
7. What if you were a cat? Cats don't write plays. Pretend you're a cat for a while.
8. Have another snack.
9. Go to the gym. Or have another snack. It's basically the same thing. Or alcohol!!

10. Wait a minute. Watch this funny video.

11. You should look something up on the internet. Like Revolutionary War uniform buttons or the names of all the Teletubbies. Or the Wombles.

12. There are more funny videos to watch. Or what about the video for the Safety Dance? That's fun. That reminds me of *Labyrinth*. Watch that. Oh, David Bowie! Sad. Let's watch all his videos on YouTube.

13. The day is almost done and you have successfully not written a play. Congratulations!

14. STOP! You were about to stay up and write a play, weren't you? Don't you have emails to respond to?

OTHER BOOKS TO READ
ABOUT WRITING AND LIVING:
AN INCOMPLETE LIST

Jackie Goldfinger's *Playwriting with Purpose*

Jackie Goldfinger and Allison Horsley's *Writing Adaptations and Translations for the Stage*

Sarah Ruhl's *100 Essays I Don't Have Time to Write: On Umbrellas and Sword Fights, Parades and Dogs, Fire Alarms, Children, and Theater*

Steven Dietz's *Doom Eager: Notes on Making Plays*

David Ball's *Backwards & Forwards: A Technical Manual for Reading Plays*

Sara Farrington's *The Lost Conversation: Interviews with an Enduring Avant-Garde*

Anne Lamont's *Bird by Bird: Some Instructions on Writing and Life*

Julia Cameron's *The Artist's Way: A Spiritual Path to Higher Creativity*

Steven Pressfield's *The War of Art: Break through the Blocks and Win Your Inner Creative Battles*

Stephen King's *On Writing*

Annie Dillard's *The Writing Life*

Lewis Hyde's *The Gift: Creativity and the Artist in the Modern World*

Robert Waldinger and Marc Schulz's *The Good Life: Lessons from the World's Longest Scientific Study of Happiness*

THAT'S IT

That's all I know. Close the book. It's over. Or, actually, I bet a month after the book is published I'll think of one other thing I should have included. I hope that, whatever it is, it isn't the one thing that would have changed your life.

Actually, there's a little more if you want to see a list of my plays and the people I thank at the end of the book.

Anyway, good luck. See you at a play, probably. When that happens, please say "Hi." The theater world is tiny. We need each other.

All best wishes,
Adam Szymkowicz

My Published Plays
as of This Moment

Marian, or The True Tale of Robin Hood: The Musical. Music and lyrics by Masi Asare. Concord/Samuel French, 2024.

Hearts Like Planets. Dramatist Play Service/Broadway Licensing, 2024.

Clown Bar Christmas. Concord/Samuel French, 2024.

The Christmas Tree Farm. Broadway Play Publishing, 2024.

Small Explosions: Bold and Combustible New Monologues for All Ages and Genders. Applause, 2023.

When Jack Met Jill. Stage Partners, 2023.

Heart of Snow. Stage Partners, 2023.

The Wooden Heart. Theatrical Rights Worldwide, 2023.

Two One-Act Plays: 100 Things I Never Said To You / 100 Love Letters I Never Sent. Concord/Samuel French, 2023.

Stockholm Syndrome. Broadway Play Publishing, 2022.

Clown Bar 2. Concord/Samuel French, 2022.

The Night Children. Playscripts, 2022.

The Bookstore. Playscripts. 2022.

Old Fashioned Cold Fusion: Short Plays about Love. Stage Partners, 2022.

Kodachrome: One-Act Version. Concord/Samuel French, 2022.

The Parking Lot. Broadway Play Publishing, 2021.

Marian, or The True Tale of Robin Hood: Teen Edition. Concord/Samuel French, 2021.

MY PUBLISHED PLAYS AS OF THIS MOMENT

Kodachrome. Concord/Samuel French, 2019.

Mercy. Concord/Samuel French, 2019.

Marian, or The True Tale of Robin Hood. Concord/Samuel French, 2017.

Rare Birds. Dramatists Play Service, 2017.

Incendiary. Broadway Play Publishing, 2017.

The Adventures of Super Margaret. Playscripts, 2016.

7 Ways to Say I Love You (seven short plays). Playscripts, 2015.

Clown Bar. Concord/Samuel French, 2014.

Hearts Like Fists. Dramatists Play Service, 2013.

The Why Overhead. Original Works Publishing, 2013.

Pretty Theft. Concord/Samuel French, 2009.

Nerve. Dramatists Play Service, 2007.

Food For Fish. Dramatists Play Service, 2007.

Deflowering Waldo. Dramatists Play Service, 2006.

More Acknowledgments

Remember when I said you should thank people as often as you can? I would like to thank all these folks and many more that I'm just not thinking about at the moment.

Special thanks in no particular order to:

John and Rhoda Szymkowicz, Seth Glewen, The Gersh Agency, Lily Creed, Poppy O'Hara. Tish Dace, Kristen Palmer, Wallace Palmer Szymkowicz, Elizabeth Bochain, John Stanizzi, Carole Shores. Betty Michel, David Michel. Ethan Harari. Bonnie Peters, Sharon Steflik.

Flux Theater Ensemble and The Chance Theater, two of my artistic homes that happen to be on opposite coasts. Thank you for all the developmental support over the years.

Joe Kraemer and The Juilliard School, Michelle Bossy and Primary Stages, Lia Romeo and Project Y, Liz Appel, Oanh Nguyen, Casey Long, James Michael McHale, Heather Cohn. Troy Heard. A.J. Allegra. Bill Taylor. Meghan Covington.

Howard Sherman.

Susan Weiss.

Andrew Compagno. Joe Reed. Karianne Kendall Rand. Nicole Davis. Tom Cleary.

Emily Rubin. Scott Ebersold. Kelly O'Donnell. Rich Orloff. Susan Louise O'Connor. Mandi Moss. Kevin R. Free. Nandita Shenoy. Rachael Hip-Flores. Nastaran Ahmadi. Sheila Callaghan. Tracy Wells. Don Zolidis. Jason Pizzarello.

MORE ACKNOWLEDGMENTS

Gwydion Suilebhan and The New Play Exchange.

Everyone at the Drama Book Shop.

Ellen Morrone.

Chris Chappell and everyone at Applause.

Judy Landman.

The many people who read this book and gave me notes. I'm sorry if I have forgotten any of you. Donna Hoke, Nia Akilah Robinson, Corinna Schulenburg, Jonathan Caren, Sophie McIntosh, Emily Hartford, Kari Bentley-Quinn, Enid Graham, Aurin Squire.

The forty or so playwrights who went through Juilliard while I was working there.

My classmates at Columbia and Juilliard and the many, many playwrights I've been in writing groups with over the years.